NEEDLEWEAVING AND EMBROIDERY:

Embellished Treasures

Effie Mitrofanis

SALLYMILNER
PUBLISHING

Dedicated to my mother, Maria,
who taught me to stitch

First published in 2005 by
Sally Milner Publishing Pty Ltd
PO Box 2104
Bowral NSW 2576
AUSTRALIA

© Effie Mitrofanis 2005

Design: Anna Warren, Warren Ventures
Diagrams: Wendy Gorton and Anna Warren
Editing: Anne Savage
Photography: Lee Sincic

Printed in China

National Library of Australia Cataloguing-in-Publication data:
Mitrofanis, Effie.
    Needleweaving and embroidery : embellished treasures.

    ISBN 1 86351 344 2.

    1. Embroidery. 2. Needlework. I. Title. (Series : Milner craft series).

    746.44

10 9 8 7 6 5 4 3 2 1

ACKNOWLEDGEMENTS

Special thanks to all the participants who have taken part in my Home Study Course of Traditional Embroidery and attended my workshops and tutorials throughout Australia and New Zealand. Their questions opened the way for me to look for answers which developed into the exploration of numerous possibilities.

To Barbara Carnie, Margery Bennett, Judith Grey, Barbara Hunt and Joan Wilson of the Miranda Group of The Embroiderer's Guild NSW, who patiently and conscientiously tested the first draft of instructions for the basic techniques—their initial input has been invaluable.

The Embroiderer's Guild NSW Inc., through which my love of creative embroidery was nurtured and developed from a hobby into a passion and a profession.

To Radda Pty Limited, for their sponsorship.

To Penny Doust from Sally Milner Publishing for her enthusiasm and guidance.

To brilliant editor Anne Savage—our third book together—whose challenging and perceptive questions have greatly improved the depth and clarity of my instructions.

To Anna Warren, talented and versatile graphic artist, who coincidentally illustrated my first book.

To Lee Sincic, photographer and teacher, for his high standards and attention to detail—our fourth book together.

To my daughters Helen and Maria, my sister Myrtle and brother-in-law Emanouel, and my brother Emmanuel for their personal support.

CONTENTS

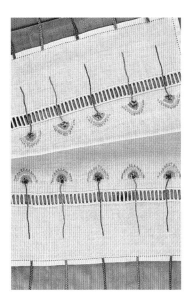

INTRODUCTION

Stitchers who have dabbled in cross stitch, hardangar and pulled work, as well as beginners and the more experienced, are invited to venture into *Needleweaving and Embroidery: Embellished Treasures*, which features a combination of my favourite embroidery techniques—needleweaving on drawn thread, and surface stitches.

Specially selected stitches and finishing touches are sampled in small, useful projects such as bookmarks, greeting cards, potpourri and glasses bags, a table mat and runner, and more. Small and medium sized projects allow skills to be developed through the creation of objects which are beautiful and useful, to keep or give as special gifts.

Discover the joy of creating distinctive threadworks by taking time out to relax from the pressures of daily responsibilities and feel the joy of creating. The rhythm of the stitches while handling threads and fabric is a soothing, meditative activity likely to develop into a preoccupation, even a passion. In these times of busy lifestyles, an hour or so set aside for embroidery may be both therapeutic and pleasurable.

From early times in Italy the art of embroidery and lace making has been referred to as *lavori femminili* or 'female works'. I trust that you will develop your skills by experimenting with the stitches and the projects while having lots of fun at the same time and turning 'works' into play.

Where to start? I suggest that you browse through the book first to get a general overview of the instructions and projects, then read Section1 on fabrics, threads and equipment which lists everything needed to do this type of embroidery. Environmental safety practices are a must, while care and pressing may be referred to as needed.

Section 2, opening up the fabric and related stitches, gives general hints for counting, isolating, cutting and withdrawing fabric threads. It shows how to make a border of open work, the simplest form of this type of embroidery, and stitches for finishing edges—antique hem, four-sided, satin and buttonhole.

Section 3 shows how to make a square-shaped open border. The interesting aspect of this shape is that a hole appears where the cut threads are pulled back to the corners, offering creative possibilities for embellishment.

Section 4 describes needlewoven patterns to fill open work borders—buttonhole triangles, woven bars, woven triangles and many others.

Section 5 has instructions for a range of stitches to enhance and complement the borders, offering endless arrangements and variations in monochrome or colour to create a lively contrast to the geometric patterns of open work.

Section 6 shows simple and attractive finishing touches to embellish projects—from practical hems to attractive trimmings in the form of twisted cords, tassels, plaited fringe, wrapped and beaded cord and knotted buttonhole insertion.

Section 7 gives ideas, patterns and instructions for many useful and decorative projects.

Where to start if you are unfamiliar with this type of embroidery or would like to review the methods? I suggest that you work through the techniques in Section 2 and make samples using the appropriate fabrics and threads while referring to the pages on general hints. Keep them in a folder for future reference or make them into projects. As you work through the instructions, jot down your own handy hints and include these with the sampler as they will prove to be a valuable guide.

Take the initiative and make your own combinations of projects, borders and stitches—and when something appears to go wrong use it as a creative opportunity to change direction, or cover it with stitching.

The most important aspect of any type of hand embroidery is to know that each stitcher makes her own unique mark because tension varies from person to person. This is a natural result of hand-made embroidery which sets it distinctly apart from machine-made objects.

Effie Mitrofanis

Section 1
Materials and equipment

FABRICS

Although specific fabrics have been suggested for each project, substitutions may be made with similar fabrics—however, any substitutions must be evenly woven. This means that they have the same number of threads per inch or centimetre in both warp and weft. These materials are available through specialty shops or mail order and Internet services.

Linen or linen and cotton mixtures are most suitable for this type of work. They are available in different 'counts', meaning the number of fabric threads per inch. Two counts are suggested in this book, 28 count (such as Zweigart Cashel linen) and 32 count (Zweigart Belfast linen), with approximately 28 and 32 fabric threads per inch.

It is natural that there will be changes in the fabric when threads are cut and withdrawn from linen and stitches applied, which results in the gathering together of fabric threads and curving of the grain. Some of these changes may be removed in the pressing process but because of the nature of the technique they are often part of the finished result.

Linen for embroidery is readily available nowadays in a wide range of colours. It is offered for sale not only by the metre (yard), approximately 140 cm (55 in) wide but also in packages known as pre-cuts, which are approximately 45 x 35 cm (17¾ x 13¾ in), and in fat quarters, measuring approximately 50 x 69 cm (19¾ x 27¼ in).

It has been my experience that dye lots and thread counts may vary slightly in manufacture, so always buy all the fabric (and threads) required for a project at the one time.

Clockwise from top left: silk fabrics for lining and table mats, embroidery frame, a variety of threads, embroidery hoops, linen fabrics

A. needles, B. thread puller,
C. quick unpick, D. awl,
E. scissors, F. tape measure,
G. pins, H. masking tape,
I. magic tape, J. tracing paper,
K. tracing pen, L. thimble

Cutting linen fabric

Carefully check the pattern measurements before cutting the fabric. I usually add about 5–8 cm (2–3 in) all around the pattern for handling and adjustments. When you are sure of the size of fabric required, cut and withdraw a thread to mark the cutting line.

Preventing frayed edges

Zigzag stitch or overlock immediately after cutting.

Working near edges

Attach strips of plain fabric 5 cm (2 in) or more wide to the edges of the linen, overlapping approximately 4 mm (⅛ in) to prevent fraying and allow hand-stitching near the edge.

THREADS

The projects in this book are made with embroidery threads that are readily available. They are DMC stranded cotton (floss) and perle. These may be substituted with space-dyed stranded cottons or floss, silks or other threads. When substituting other products, the thickness of the thread and its scale in relation to the stitch and fabric should be considered. Small samples may need to be worked first to test their relationship and effectiveness. Consideration must also be given to the use of the article and laundering needs.

Separating stranded cottons and silks

Separating six-stranded cottons or stranded silks before stitching is recommended for some stitches as it results in better cover of thread on fabric and prevents multiple strands from twisting and tangling. Attach the needle and thread to the starting point in the usual way and push the needle back along the thread until it rests on the surface of the fabric. Insert a tapestry needle between the strands near the surface of the fabric and, while holding them together with one hand, separate one strand at a time, pulling it away from the group with the other hand.

EQUIPMENT

Light

It is important for any type of embroidery that good lighting is used, either daylight or an adjustable lamp focused on the work. If the work cannot be done without eyestrain, it may mean that a check-up is indicated.

Needles

The following types are recommended for this type of work:

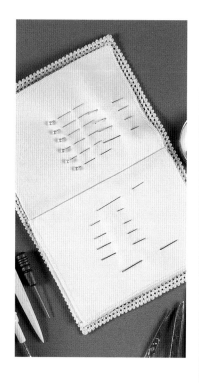

- **Tapestry needles** have a large eye and a blunt point that will not split the threads of the fabric, making them ideal for use in linen embroidery where the needle must separate the fabric threads and pass through the holes of the fabric. They are suitable for antique hem stitch, four-sided stitch and woven stitches and come in sizes 16–26: the smaller the number the larger the size. Use size 24 for 5 and 8 perle and stranded cotton.

- **Crewel or embroidery needles** have sharp points and are suitable for surface stitches such as chain, buttonhole and French knots. They have a long narrow eye to carry the thread and facilitate ease of passage through the fabric with minimum thread irritation and come in sizes 3–9, again the smallest number referring to the largest size.

- **Milliners/straw needles** are ideal for bullion stitch as they are long and smooth.

Needle hints

Never use rusty needles—throw them away! Prevent rusting by storing packets of needles in an airtight container and single needles in a needle-book of doctor flannel or felt. The right needle for the purpose makes the embroidery easier and results in a better finish. Choose the right size for the thickness used and the right type, that is, pointed or blunt end, to suit the thread, fabric and stitch.

If the needle is not passing easily through the fabric and is causing damage to the embroidery thread, change to a larger needle which will create a hole in the fabric big enough to allow it to pass through smoothly. If the needle is too large it could distort the fabric or result in unwanted gaps between stitches. Another way to minimise thread damage is to change the position of the needle on the thread from time to time and let it hang loosely to unravel twists.

Embroidery hoop

The inner ring of the hoop should be bound with bias binding or cotton tape to keep the work firm and clean and stop the hoop from slipping. I find hoops from approximately 13 to 17 cm (5–7 in) in diameter hold the fabric in place while allowing good tension control and easy access for stitching in the centre of the hoop. The screw of the hoop should be tightened to firm tension so that the fabric is held straight. The fabric should not remain in the hoop for long periods, not even overnight, as this may stretch or distort the linen. Right-handers place the screw at 10 o'clock when working, left-handers at 2 o'clock.

Other requirements

- **Sharp, fine-pointed embroidery scissors** are important as they are needed for isolating and cutting fabric threads.

- **Fabric scissors** Larger, sharp scissors are used for cutting fabric.

- **Thread puller or stitch fixer** A handy tool to facilitate withdrawing fabric threads after they have been cut as it provides leverage. Make your own with a size 18 tapestry needle pushed into a cork.

- **Awl** A small pointed tool for piercing and stretching holes in the fabric.

- **Tape measure or ruler** For measuring.

- **Pins** Fine, clean pins for counting and securing fabric in place.

- **Masking tape** approximately 2 cm (1 in) wide or **magic Sellotape** For holding loose withdrawn fabric threads in place until they are secured with stitching.

- **Tracing paper** Kitchen greaseproof paper is suitable for tracing designs when transferring them to fabric.

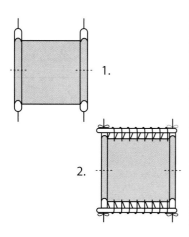

Lacing fabric to an embroidery frame

- **Embroidery frame** Some projects are easier to stitch when the fabric is mounted onto an embroidery frame. The frame should be large enough that the whole working area is visible.

1   Mark the centre points on two sides of the fabric with pins. Mark the centres of the rollers with pen or pencil. Pin the fabric to the roller tape, matching the centre marks. Stitch fabric to roller tape with a wide, long machine zigzag. Attach the cross-bars and screw them in place.

2   Using fine, soft string or 4-ply non-stretch knitting/crochet cotton (not sewing cotton), lace the fabric to the cross-bars. Use a continuous length of yarn on each side. Make sure that the fabric is straight and parallel to the bars before tying off the lacing thread. Tighten the rollers, and adjust them as needed while stitching.

TRANSFERRING THE DESIGN TO FABRIC

Tacking around cut-out paper shapes This method is quick and easy for transferring solid shapes. Trace the design onto tracing paper and pin it in place on the fabric. Run-stitch around the edges with sewing cotton in a contrasting colour, making sure that details such as corners are clearly recorded. The tacking stitches may be stitched over, pulled out or cut away.

Fabric pens Care needs to be taken when using washable fabric transfer pens. Apply a fine or dotted line rather than a thick, solid one. After transferring the design to the fabric, do not allow heat or sunlight onto the fabric until the pen has been washed out as it may remain.

ENVIRONMENTAL SAFETY

- Keep pins and needles safely in a container, a pincushion or a needle-book. Never place pins or needles in the mouth.

- Don't walk barefoot in a sewing area.

- Always cut threads with scissors, not teeth.

- Wash hands before handling materials but don't apply hand cream unless it is specifically recommended for embroiderers.

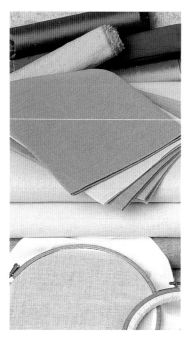

- When using glue, work in an open area or outside. It is recommended that a lightweight mask, available from hardware stores, be worn. Read instructions on how to use products.

- Sharp-bladed cutting knives should only be used with great care and full attention. Always cut alongside a metal ruler, making a number of light strokes rather than heavy ones.

LAUNDERING, PRESSING AND STORING EMBROIDERY

Laundering

The following washing procedure is recommended.

Hand-wash each piece gently and separately in warm to cool water using pure or mild soap. Avoid using a detergent with a blueing or bleaching agent.

During the washing, if the water becomes coloured, continue to wash with cold water and rinse thoroughly several times. Hold the embroidery right side downwards and allow the rinsing water to flow through from the back

Roll in a thick towel to remove moisture.

While still slightly damp, place the stitched side face down onto a towel with a pressing cloth over the back of the work. Avoid steam on the embroidery. Avoid dry cleaning.

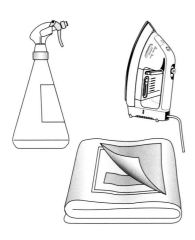

Equipment for pressing embroidery—iron, spray bottle, thick towel, pressing cloth

Pressing

To retain linen's crisp appearance it needs to be ironed while damp. It is very important, when pressing embroidery, to watch the temperature of the iron—if it's too hot it may burn or singe the work; too cool, it may crease or dirty the fabric. Use the temperature setting recommended by the manufacturer for the particular fabric and test the iron on a spare piece of the fabric.

Place embroidery face down onto a thick, clean bath towel which has been folded several times. Immediately before pressing spray a fine mist of water onto the back of the work. You may cover it with a lightweight pressing cloth or a large cotton handkerchief. Press slowly and evenly, following the straight grain of the fabric, using the other hand to arrange and adjust the damp fabric. If the fabric is slightly out of shape it may be gently stretched into shape and pinned onto the ironing board while it is still damp.

Starching

Starching and stiffening embroidery is a matter of personal taste. Traditional starch is still available in some stores. It is dissolved in cold water so that it becomes milky. The wet or dry embroidery is dipped into this, then squeezed well while flat (don't twist or wring), and wrapped in a clean cloth for an hour before being pressed with a hot iron. Dry fabric will absorb more starch than wet fabric so it is wise to experiment following the manufacturer's instructions. Boiled starch is used when a much greater degree of stiffening is required.

Ironing aids and spray starch may also be used.

Storing embroidery

- The best way to store small pieces of embroidery is to lay them flat. Larger pieces should be wrapped around a cylinder covered with acid-free tissue paper.

- Always launder soiled embroidery before storing.

- For old and special items consult an expert.

- Change fold lines regularly on larger pieces.

- Airing embroideries from time to time helps to keep them fresh.

Section 2
Borders of open work

HINTS AND TIPS

Place fabric in hoop or frame before counting, cutting and withdrawing. Keep track of the numbers of fabric threads by counting in groups of 10 and inserting a pin in the holes to mark the divisions. Count fabric threads, not holes.

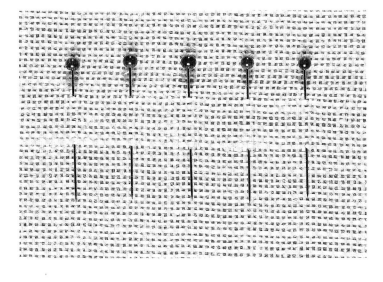

Counting threads using pins

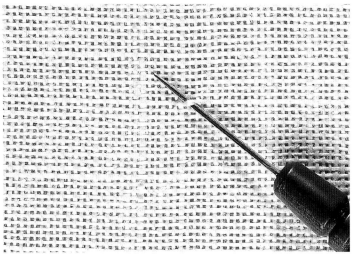

Isolating a thread to be cut

Isolating a thread to be cut

Select the fabric thread to be cut and isolate it with a tapestry needle or thread puller. Push fabric forward from the back with one finger to facilitate selection of fabric thread. With one blade of the fine-pointed, sharp embroidery scissors, pick up the fabric thread to be cut. PAUSE. Check that the correct thread has been picked up, pull it out a little, then cut.

Immediately pull out the fabric thread for 2 cm (¾ in), so that it is easily seen.

Start at the top of the shape, cutting one thread at a time, pointing scissors towards the fabric threads already cut and away from the worker.

Cutting fabric threads within a border

back of work

Cut threads are withdrawn to the edge of the fabric and held down with tape at the back of the work

To withdraw cut fabric threads to the edges, use a stitch fixer or tapestry needle to pull all threads for small distances, approximately 2 cm (1 in) at a time, rather than pulling one thread the whole distance. To assist in identifying a single thread as it is being pulled, give it a firm tug so that it stands out from the others. Pull the fabric threads to the edge of the border at the back and hold them with tape.

Beginning to stitch

Start with a waste knot. This is a knot tied or made at the end of embroidery thread and cut off after use. Insert the needle 8 cm (3 in) away from the starting point. When stitching is complete cut off the waste knot and stitch the tail into the back.

Finish embroidery threads by weaving or whipping around stitches at the back.

Repairing inadvertently cut vertical threads

Finish dividing the border into groups. Stitch the ends of the cut vertical thread into the back of the work with matching coloured sewing cotton. Thread a length of linen thread from the edge or from spare fabric into a tapestry needle and, starting with a waste knot, stitch it through the back of one edge for 2–3 cm (1 in), then across the open area, finishing off through the back of the opposite edge, as indicated by the dotted line in the picture.

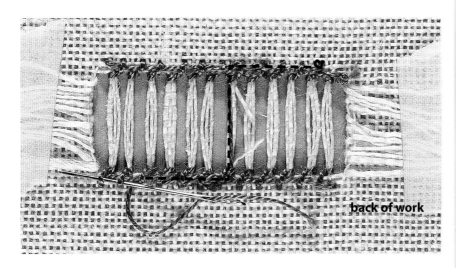

back of work

Repairing a damaged vertical thread, here demonstrated with a contrasting colour

Replacing an incorrectly cut fabric thread

Weave a length of linen thread into the fabric where the thread has been cut, weaving beyond the ends of the gap for 3–4 cm (1½ in).

Embroidery hints

If the needle is not passing easily through the fabric and is causing fraying and thread damage, change to a larger needle which makes a hole big enough to allow the thread to pass through easily.

If the needle is too large it could distort the fabric or result in unwanted gaps between stitches.

Minimise thread damage by changing the position of the needle on the thread from time to time.

Beginning and ending a thread

Tie a waste knot (cut off after use) at the end of the thread and take the needle and thread from the top to the back of the fabric 8 cm (3 in) away from the starting point, and commence stitching. When stitching is complete cut off the waste knot and stitch the end into the back of the work. To finish a thread, stitch it under and around previous work at the back.

Correcting excess or under-counted threads into required groups

Don't despair or unpick. If fabric threads aren't quite enough to make up the number of required groups, divide one or more groups with fewer threads than the number specified, for example, 2 threads instead of 3, or 3 threads instead of 4.

If there are too many fabric threads for the number of required groups, incorporate an extra thread into one or more groups, for example, 4 threads instead of 3, or 5 threads instead of 4.

When multiple borders of open work are required, as in the book cover, sampler panel and potpourri bag or glasses case, I suggest the following order of working—count, pin-mark and tack the approximate placement of each row in position on the fabric. Complete each border row by row, cutting and withdrawing fabric

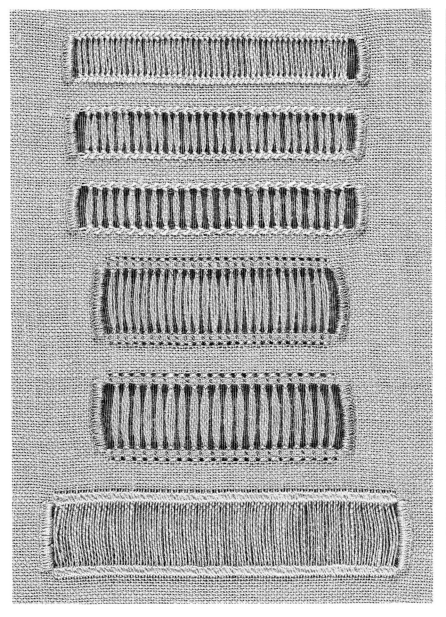

Borders of open work:

1. Antique hem stitch dividing fabric threads into groups of 2, with perle 8

2. Antique hem stitch dividing fabric threads into groups of 3, with perle 8

3. Antique hem stitch dividing fabric threads into groups of 4, with perle 8

4. Four-sided stitch dividing fabric threads into groups of 3, with perle 8

5. Four-sided stitch dividing fabric threads into groups of 4, with perle 8

6. Satin stitch border in perle 5 or 8

All short edges are secured with 3 strands cotton with buttonhole stitch.

threads and dividing them into groups, needleweaving the patterns and lastly buttonhole-stitching the short edges.

OPEN WORK EDGED WITH ANTIQUE HEM STITCH

Antique hem stitch divides fabric threads into groups of 2, 3 or 4 depending on the type of decorative fillings, the scale and the desired effect. It is worked with perle 8, or 2 or 3 strands of cotton 75 cm (30 in) long in a size 24 tapestry needle. Start with a waste knot (cut off after use) and finish off by threading under stitches at the back. Resulting measurements may vary depending on the count and weave of the fabric used.

MATERIALS

Belfast or other even weave fabric

DMC perle 8, colour to match fabric

DMC stranded cotton, colour to match fabric

Tapestry needle size 24

Embroidery or crewel needle size 5 or 7

Embroidery hoop

INSTRUCTIONS

In this example antique hem stitch is used to divide the fabric threads into groups of 3.

Choose an area of fabric on which to work a border (indicated by the broken lines in Fig. 1), approximately 42 threads wide and 14 threads deep. Select a horizontal fabric thread in the centre at the base, A, and cut it. Ease the cut thread out of the fabric, to the left of the centre to corner B, and hold it with tape at the back. The first side of the border is now ready for antique hem stitch.

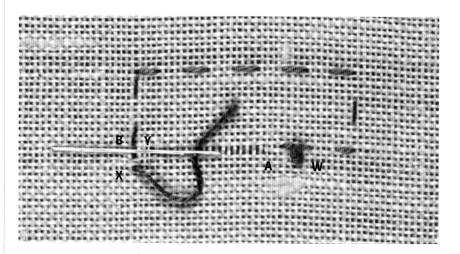

Fig. 1 Antique hem stitch dividing fabric threads into groups of 3

Step 1 Take the needle and thread from the front to the back into the fabric at W, 8 cm (3 in) away from B and 2 fabric threads below withdrawn thread A-B. Bring the needle and thread out at the front through hole X, 2 fabric threads below corner B. Place the working thread BELOW the position of the next stitch, towards you, and hold it with your thumb while placing the needle from right to left behind a group of 3 fabric threads, X-Y-B. Pull the thread through to the front with medium to firm tension.

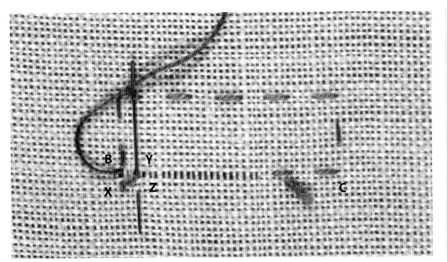

Fig. 2 Antique hem stitch dividing fabric threads into groups of 3

Step 2 See Fig. 2. Place the working thread ABOVE the position of the next stitch, away from you, and take the needle to the back through the space Y made in step 1. Push it from the back to the front, out through a hole two fabric threads below Y at Z, with medium to firm tension. Z is on the same line as X. (Make sure this stitch is worked over the starting thread at the back.) Repeat antique hem stitch across the area to the middle of the shape and withdraw the cut thread from A to corner C.

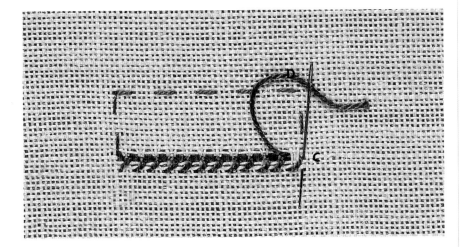

Fig. 3 Antique hem stitch dividing fabric threads into groups of 3

See Fig. 3. Continue dividing the fabric threads into groups of 3 to the edge of the shape. Take step 2 of the last stitch into the corner at C and finish off through the back of the stitches, or run stitch from C to D, to be covered later with buttonhole stitch.

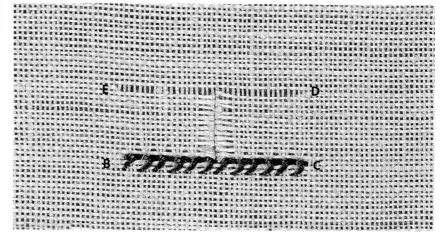

Fig. 4 Antique hem stitch dividing fabric threads into groups of 3

See Fig. 4. Open the border by cutting 14 horizontal fabric threads in the centre, selecting and cutting one at a time. The top of the border is D-E.

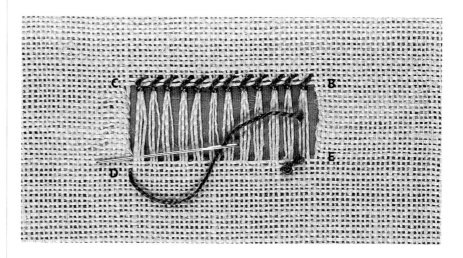

Fig. 5 Antique hem stitch dividing fabric threads into groups of 3

See Fig. 5. Pull the cut threads back to the sides of the border and hold them in place at the back with tape.

Turn the work upside down so that the bottom edge of the border B-C, now worked with antique hem stitch, is at the top and the top D-E now becomes the base. Work antique hem stitch between D and E and finish off.

The short edges are now ready to be secured with buttonhole stitch.

SECURING EDGES WITH DECORATIVE STITCHES

Buttonhole stitch

Step 1 Using 3 strands cotton in an embroidery needle, backstitch the edge A-B to hold the loose fabric threads. Work buttonhole stitch from A to B, entering the fabric 4 or 5 fabric threads away from the opening. To create a smooth, looped edge of buttonhole stitches, tension the thread very firmly by pulling it level with the fabric.

Step 2 Work buttonhole stitches as follows for even spacing and tension: As the stitch is tensioned, insert the needle into the loop and guide it into place close to the previous stitch. Pull the thread firmly, level with the fabric, then remove the needle from the loop while continuing to hold the thread at tension as the next stitch is made.

Step 3 Finish off the thread through the back of the stitches. Cut away excess fabric threads and the tape at the back.

Buttonhole stitch the opposite side in the same way.

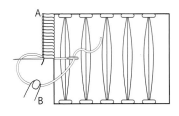

Buttonhole stitch, step 1

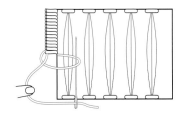

Buttonhole stitch, step 2

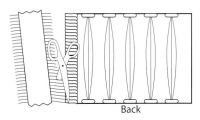

Buttonhole stitch, step 3

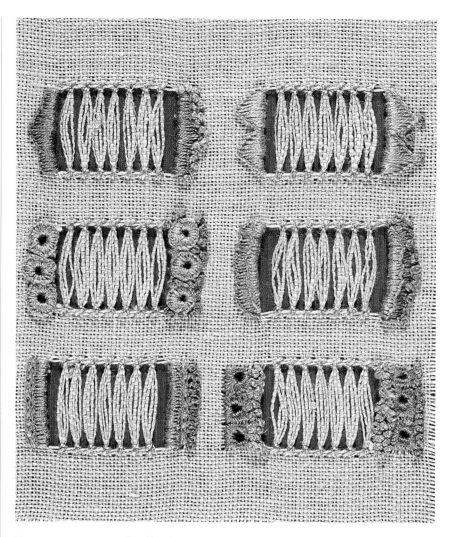

Decorative embellishments

Buttonholed edges embellished in more dramatic ways:

Top row Shaped buttonhole stitch on the edges, with French knots added on the right edge

Middle row On the left, buttonhole eyelets with French knots; on the right, a narrow row of buttonhole stitch on top of a wider row of buttonhole stitch, with French knots added on the right edge

Bottom row On the left, chain stitch and French knots are added to buttonhole stitch; on the right, French knots are worked over buttonhole stitch and square eyelets added outside the knots, with more knots on the right edge

FOUR-SIDED STITCH

Four-sided stitch is a very popular and commonly used stitch in open work

Prepare fabric by withdrawing one horizontal fabric thread, leave 3, withdraw another one, both shown as shaded lines in the diagrams.

Three steps are repeated from right to left (left-handers mirror image) between the two withdrawn horizontal fabric threads with medium to firm tension. Note that all stitches at the back are diagonal.

Step 1 Starting with a waste knot on the end of the thread, take the needle and thread from the front to the back into the fabric at W, 8 cm (3 in) away from A, in the space between the withdrawn threads, and bring the needle out at A. Push needle down into B, 3 fabric threads vertical to A, and out at C, 4 fabric threads horizontal to A.

Step 2 Insert needle into A and out at D, 4 fabric threads horizontal to the left of B.

Step 3 Insert needle into B and out at C.

Repeat these three steps, ensuring that the starting thread is covered with stitches at the back. Cut off the waste knot as it is reached.

To change thread midstream take the thread forward 8 cm (3 in) in the middle of the border after working step 3, B-E. Start the new thread as described in step 1. The diagram shows each four-sided stitch as 3 fabric threads deep and 4 wide. It may also be worked over 3 fabric threads deep and 3 wide, as seen in the woven triangles book cover, to accommodate some needlewoven patterns.

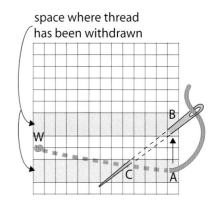

space where thread has been withdrawn

Step 1

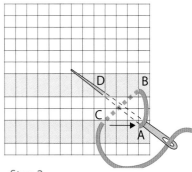

Step 2

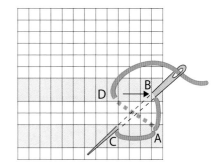

Step 3

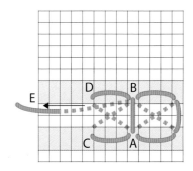

Changing thread midstream

OPEN WORK EDGED WITH FOUR-SIDED STITCH

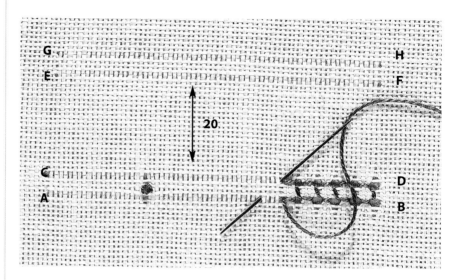

Withdrawing the border lines and working four-sided stitch

Lower border In the middle of the border, select and cut a horizontal fabric thread and pull it back to the edges A-B. Count 3 fabric threads above A-B and withdraw the next, to make C-D the same width.

The area between these two lines is worked with four-sided stitch with perle 8 or 2–3 strands cotton in a size 24 tapestry needle.

Upper border Directly above the centre of C-D count the desired number of fabric threads, 20 in this example, and cut the next fabric thread, pulling it back for the same width as A-B, to make E-F.

Count 3 fabric threads above E-F and cut the fourth fabric thread, pulling it back to the edge to form G-H.

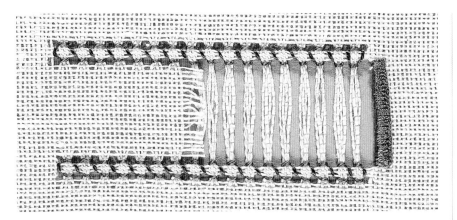

Removing horizontal fabric threads

Between the border lines, cut the horizontal fabric threads in the centre and pull them back to the sides, holding them at the back with tape.

Turn the work so that the lower border is on top and work four-sided stitch exactly opposite the groups of stitches made on the other side.

Secure the short edges with buttonhole stitch.

OPEN WORK EDGED WITH SATIN STITCH

Both sides of the border are worked with satin stitch BEFORE the fabric threads in the centre are cut and pulled back. Work with perle 5 or 8, or 3–6 strands cotton in a size 24 tapestry needle.

In the middle of the border, select and cut a horizontal fabric thread and pull it back to the edges, A-B. Count 3 fabric threads above A-B and withdraw the next, to make C-D the same width. The area between these two lines is worked with satin stitch, shown as I-J-K. Make one stitch I-J vertically between each pair of holes, coming out the hole next to I, at K. Repeat.

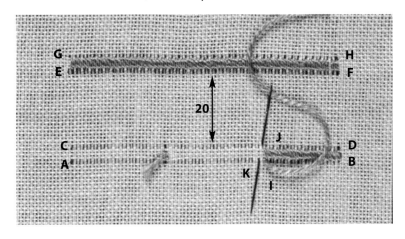

Withdrawing the border lines and stitching

29

Upper border Directly above the centre of C-D count the desired number of fabric threads, 20 in this example, and cut the next fabric thread, pulling it back for the same width as A-B, to make E-F.

Count 3 fabric threads above E-F and cut the fourth fabric thread, pulling it back to the edge to form G-H. The area between these two lines is worked with satin stitch.

Cut the horizontal fabric threads in the centre of the border and pull them back to the sides, holding them in place with tape. Secure the short edges with buttonhole stitch.

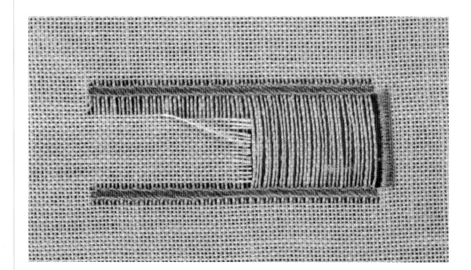

Removing horizontal fabric threads

Section 3
Square border of open work edged with antique hem stitch

A square border is made by cutting and withdrawing threads between an inner square and an outer square and working with antique hem stitch to divide the fabric threads into groups of 2, 3 or 4. When the cut threads are withdrawn, a hole results in each corner; the loose threads are held in place at the back with tape until secured with buttonhole stitch.

In this example the fabric threads are divided into groups of 3 and each side of the inner square contains 16 groups of 3 fabric threads, a total of 48 fabric threads.

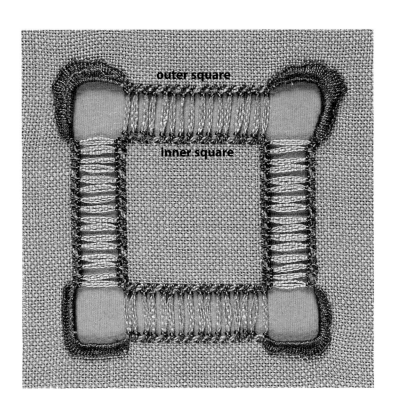

Finished border

31

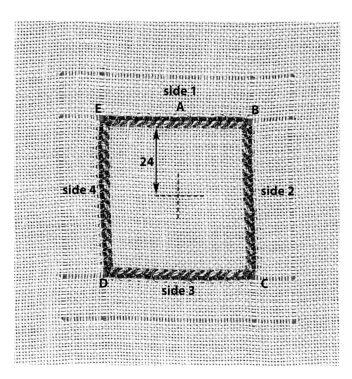

Inner square

Inner square

Mark the centre of the fabric with a cross of running stitches.

Side 1 Above the centre, count HALF the number of fabric threads required to make the inner square, in this example 24, and pin-mark at A. Cut and withdraw the 25th thread and pull it to the right, towards corner B, for approximately 25 fabric threads.

Work 7 groups of antique hem stitch from A towards B, starting 2 fabric threads below A and separating the threads into groups of 3.

Make step 1 only of the eighth and last group before turning corner B.

Turning a corner

Before working step 2 on the eighth group, cut and withdraw the next fabric thread at corner B, 2 cm (¾ in) below it, and at a right angle to side 1. Pull it back a few threads past corner B and make step 2 through the hole at corner B and out to the front through a hole 2 fabric threads inside the withdrawn thread at X in the diagram. The shaded lines are the spaces remaining after threads are withdrawn.

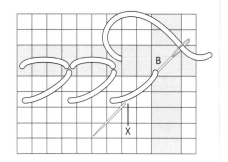

Turning a corner

Note The last stitch before turning a corner is made in the same way whether dividing fabric threads into groups of 2, 3 or 4 threads.

Side 2 Turn the work so that the next side is horizontal and, working from left to right, make step 1 of antique hem stitch around the first 3 fabric threads and including the corner hole B. Continue working antique hem stitch for a total of 16 groups of 3 fabric threads to the next corner, C, and turn it as described for corner B above.

Sides 3 and 4 Work antique hem stitch making 16 groups of 3 fabric threads on each side. When you get to corner E, pull the first fabric thread previously cut at A back to corner E, and work antique hem stitch to meet up with A. Take the last stitch to the back and finish the thread through the back of the stitches.

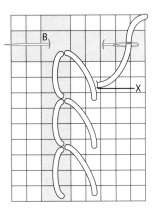

Turning a corner.
Working side 2

Outer square, sides 1–4

Starting at A, the centre of side 1 of the inner square, count 12 fabric threads to F, directly above it. Cut the 13th thread and withdraw it to meet the other sides at the corners. Repeat for the other three sides of the square.

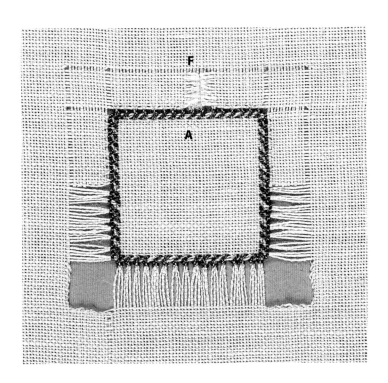

Outer square, sides 1–4.
Withdrawing fabric threads
within borders

Between the inner and outer squares, cut the fabric threads at the centre of each of the four sides and pull them out to the corners at the back of the work, holding them at the back with tape. Complete one side before you move on to the next.

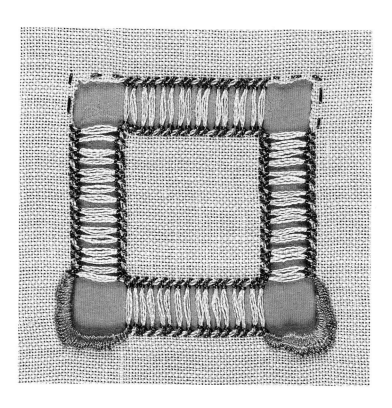

Four-sided square border with antique hem stitch completed, two square ends finished with buttonhole stitch

Work antique hem stitch dividing the fabric threads into groups of 3, directly opposite the groups of the inner square. Secure the unworked edges of the open corner squares with buttonhole stitch.

Section 4
Open work patterns

WOVEN BARS

Woven bars may be worked on open borders edged with either antique hem stitch, satin stitch or four-sided stitch. They are made by weaving two or more groups of vertical fabric threads together with perle 5 or 8, or 3 strands cotton.

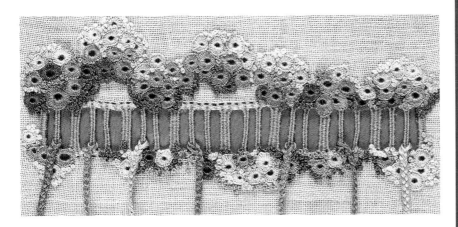

Detail of sachet project (page 99) showing woven bars in an open border worked over two and three groups of threads

To start, bring the needle out to the front in the space between two groups of vertical fabric threads at A. Take the needle over and under, back and forth over the two groups, and as you weave push the rows close together with the needle and pull the tension of each row firmly. Repeat until the two groups are covered. To facilitate weaving place the index or middle finger of the non-stitching hand under the groups as you weave, and turn the work as needed. At the end of the bar take the last stitch to the back and pass the needle and thread under the stitches at the border's edge to the next bar.

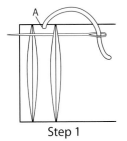

Step 1

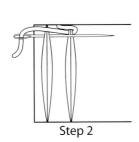

Step 2

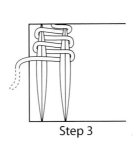

Step 3

Weaving two groups

35

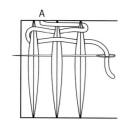

Weaving three or more groups

Choose the number of groups you wish to weave together and bring the needle to the front between two of the groups. Weave the thread back and forth, under and over all of them. Tension and pack the rows together as described above.

WOVEN TRIANGLES

Woven triangles may be worked on open borders edged with either antique hem stitch, satin stitch or four-sided stitch, over groups containing 3 or 4 vertical fabric threads, using perle 5 or 8.

I suggest you work this woven triangle as a sample. Prepare a border 39 fabric threads wide and 20 deep, edged with antique hem stitch dividing the threads into groups of 3 with perle 8. Work the triangle in perle 5. To start, bring the needle and thread to the front between the edge and the first group of vertical fabric threads at A.

Weave four rows over and under 13 groups of fabric threads, then four rows over and under 11 groups, nine, seven, five and three groups. Finally, whip around the last group and finish the thread through the back of the antique hem stitches at the edge of the border.

This detail from the bookmark with woven triangle (page 71) shows a triangle woven over 13 groups of 3 vertical threads

HINTS Facilitate ease of weaving by placing the index or middle finger of the non-stitching hand under the groups being woven, and turn the work around as needed.

Push the rows close together with the needle as you weave each row.

Tension should be reasonably firm; the shape may vary depending on personal tension. Spread the rows evenly by adjusting them with the needle.

Keep track of the number of rows by making a note of where the weaving begins, and always decrease at the same end.

When working a design with a number of woven triangles, start each one with a new thread.

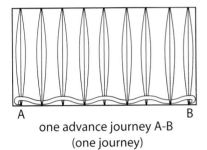

one advance journey A-B
(one journey)

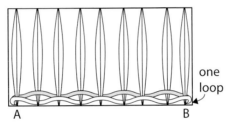

one advance and one return
journey A-B-A (two journeys)
produce one loop at each end
and one solid line of weaving A B

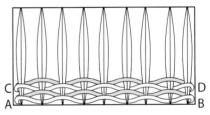

two advance and two return
journeys (four journeys) produce
two loops at each end and two
solid lines of weaving A B, C D

Working a woven triangle

One solid line of weaving is created by two journeys, one advance and one return journey, and is represented at the end of each row by ONE loop only. Two loops together at the ends of the rows represent four journeys.

To finish with a point wrapped around one group of fabric threads, the triangle must be woven over an odd number of groups. Weaving a triangle over an even number results in the point being woven over two groups.

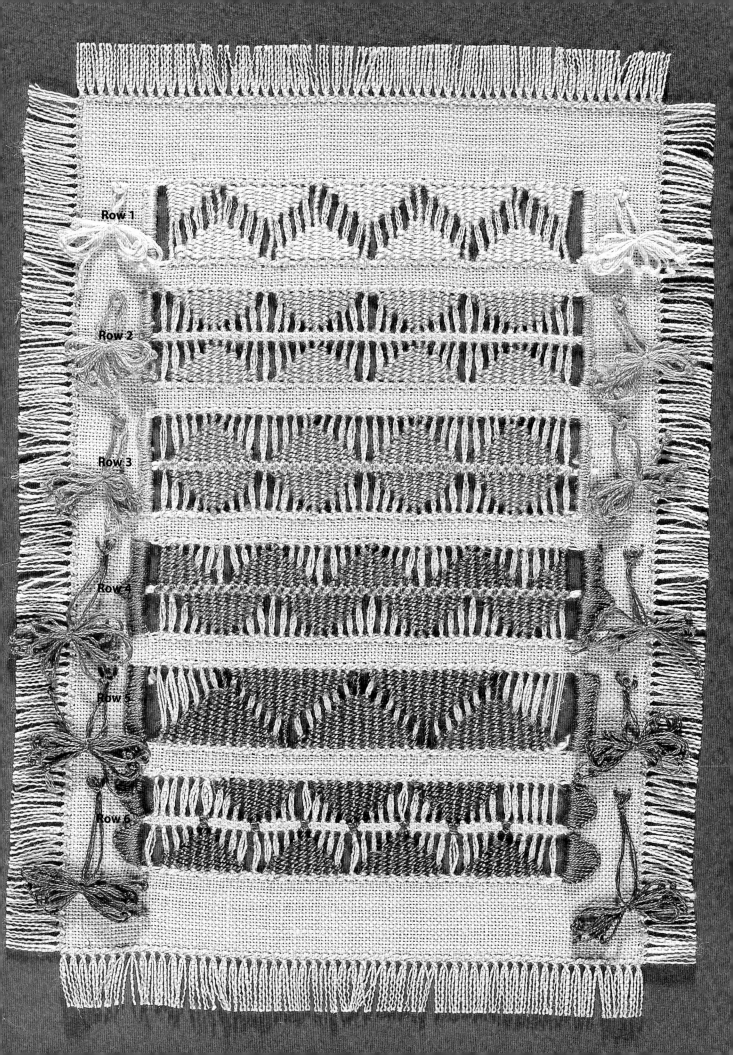

Row 1

Row 2

Row 3

Row 4

Row 5

Row 6

WOVEN TRIANGLES BOOK COVER

MATERIALS

*30 x 25 cm (12 x 10 in) Belfast linen, 32 count, colour 322
fawn or ecru*

1 ball DMC perle 8, colour 738 or ecru

1 skein each DMC stranded cotton and perle 8:

> *ecru*
> *208 lavender*
> *333 blue violet*
> *976 golden brown medium*
> *977 golden brown light*
> *3687 mauve*

Needles:

> *tapestry size 24*
> *embroidery or crewel size 5 or 7*

Embroidery frame (preferable) or hoop

Finished size 24 x 17.5 cm (9½ x 7 in)

INSTRUCTIONS

Attach fabric to the frame or attach plain fabric to the sides of the linen for use with the hoop. The format of the panel is long and narrow.

Mark the vertical and horizontal centres of the fabric with run stitching as shown in the diagram.

All borders are 123 fabric threads wide divided into 41 groups of 3 with antique hem stitch or four-sided stitch. All rows are counted 61 fabric threads to the left of the vertical centre and 62 to the right of the vertical centre.

Woven triangles book cover
with a variety of designs

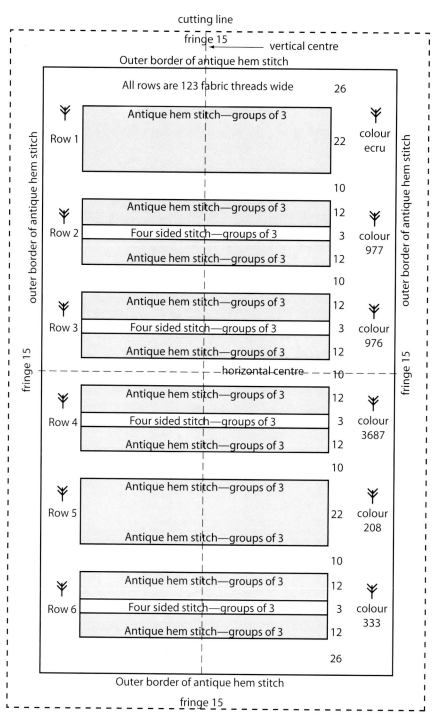

Layout of book cover
(not to scale)

String of knots attached with 2 fly (open chain) stitches

OPENING AND STITCHING THE BORDERS

Start counting from the horizontal centre mark upwards and work row 3 first.

Row 3 Count 5 fabric threads up from the horizontal centre and withdraw 12 fabric threads deep and 123 wide, leave 3 (to be worked with four-sided stitch), withdraw another 12 fabric threads deep, 123 wide.

Divide one edge into 41 groups of 3 fabric threads with antique hem stitch using perle 8.

Work four-sided stitch over the 3 fabric threads in the centre of the border dividing them into GROUPS of 3 exactly opposite the antique hem stitch.

Repeat antique hem stitch on the other side of the border, exactly opposite the four-sided stitch.

Row 2 Leave 10 fabric threads and work the same as row 3.

Row 1 Leave 10 fabric threads and withdraw 22 fabric threads deep, 123 wide. Divide fabric threads into groups of 3 exactly opposite each other.

Row 4 Leave 10 fabric threads below Row 3 and work the same as row 3.

Row 5 Leave 10 fabric threads and work same as row 1.

Row 6 Leave 10 fabric threads and work the same as row 3.

WOVEN TRIANGLE BORDERS

Start each triangle with a new thread. As you finish the triangles in each border, work buttonhole stitch over the short ends of the border with 3 strands cotton in the same colour.

Each descending level of the triangles is worked with 4 rows of weaving, that is, two advance and two return journeys (as in the detail photograph of woven triangles on page 36). The difference is that each triangle may start over a different number of groups and contain less or more descending levels. The depth of the border is also relative to the size of the triangle, for which there are no pre-set measurements, only trial and error to discover a pleasing balance of proportion.

Row 1 Perle 5 ecru woven triangles over 9 groups; one group of threads between each triangle is left unworked to take the point of the opposite triangle.

Row 2 Perle 5 colour 977 woven triangles over 9 groups, one group at the beginning and end of the row and between each triangle left unworked, same as row 1, except that the triangles are worked opposite each other with the peaks pointing to the centre.

Row 3 Perle 5 colour 976, same as row 2 except the bases of the triangles start in the centre. One group at the beginning and end of the lower side is left unworked.

Row 4 Perle 5 colour 3687 woven triangles over 9 groups, arranged to form a zigzag line. One group between each triangle and 2 groups at the beginning of the lower side are left unworked.

Row 5 Perle 5 colour 208 woven triangles over 13 groups, one group between each left unworked to take the point of the opposite triangle. Start on the lower side with three triangles.

Row 6 Perle 5 colour 333; each woven triangle over 9 groups, one group between each left unworked to take the point of the opposite triangle. One group at the beginning and end of the lower side is also left unworked, and 6 groups at the beginning and end of the upper side. Each triangle finishes in the centre with a cross stitch.

Outer border of antique hem stitch Count 26 fabrics threads out from the borders on all sides and withdraw 1 fabric thread. Work antique hem stitch with perle 8, holding the edge of the fabric away from you.

Fringe Count 15 fabric threads away from the borders on all four sides and withdraw the 16th. This is the cutting line. Cut on this line to remove excess fabric and remove fabric threads to form the fringe.

Strings of knots Make 2 strings of knots in each colour and attach to the sides of the borders with 2 open chain stitches (fly stitch).

Finishing Stitch the embroidery with sewing cotton to coloured card with edges torn. To tear the card, fold it on the line to be torn and apply a little water with a sponge to the back of it. Place a ruler on the fold and gently tear it. Glue the card with the embroidery to the cover of a book, diary, journal or address book.

BUTTONHOLE TRIANGLES

Buttonhole triangles are worked on open borders edged with antique hem stitch dividing vertical fabric threads into groups of 2 or 3.

Different patterns are created by pointing the triangles all the same way or by mirror-imaging them.

Tension on the buttonhole stitches should be reasonably firm, but their shape may vary depending on your personal tension. Spread the stitches evenly by adjusting them with the needle as you work. To prevent the knotted edge of the buttonhole stitch from rolling inwards pull the thread level with the fabric and hold it there until the next buttonhole stitch is pulled through.

To practise 3 triangles of this technique, prepare an open border 36 fabric threads wide and 12 deep, divided into 18 groups of 2 with antique hem stitch using perle 8 or 3 strands cotton in a size 24 tapestry needle.

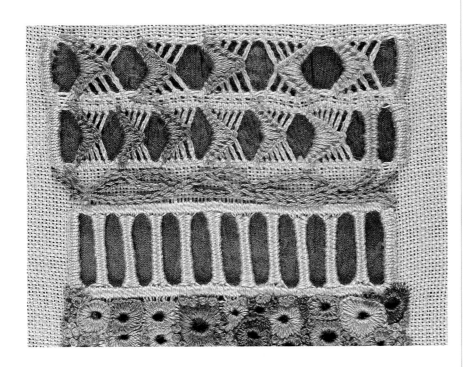

Detail of the border of buttonhole triangles from the sampler panel (page 77)

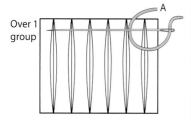

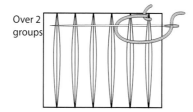

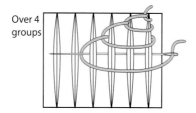

Fig. 1 Using 3 strands cotton in a size 24 tapestry needle, bring the needle and thread out through the fabric, 2 fabric threads below the edge of the first group, that is, the same hole as the antique hem stitch, A, and make one buttonhole stitch over one group of fabric threads.

Fig. 2 Make the second stitch around 2 groups.

Fig. 3 Make the third stitch around 3 groups.

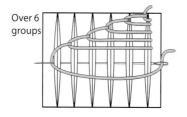

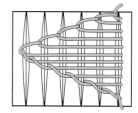

Fig. 4 Make the fourth stitch around 4 groups.

Fig. 5 Make the fifth stitch around 5 groups.

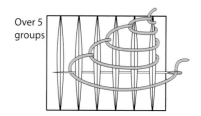

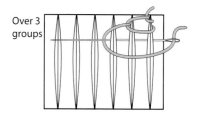

Fig. 6 Make the sixth stitch around 6 groups. This stitch forms the point of the triangle.

Fig. 7 Complete the triangle by working one buttonhole stitch over 5, 4, 3, 2 and 1 groups of fabric threads. Finish off by taking the needle and thread down into the second fabric thread below the edge, directly opposite the starting point.

Take the needle and thread to the next triangle through the back of the border. Finish off threads through stitches at the back.

Buttonhole triangle variation

For the next example, prepare a border 18 fabric threads wide and 20 deep, divided into groups of 3 with antique hem stitch, using perle 5 in a tapestry needle. This is worked in the same way as above except there are four buttonhole stitches over 6 groups instead of one stitch over 6 groups (Fig. 8).

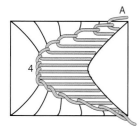

Fig. 8 Buttonhole triangle variation worked in border 18 fabric threads wide and 20 deep divided into groups of 3

WRAPPED BARS AND NEEDLEWOVEN PATTERNS

Wrapped and needlewoven patterns enhance open work borders. A specific border may be planned before it is opened and the fabric threads divided into groups, or a pattern may be designed after the border is opened.

Design your own borders by combining different patterns and one, two or more wrapped bars. When groups of fabric threads in a border do not divide evenly to fit a particular pattern, you can add wrapped or woven bars to cover the remaining groups.

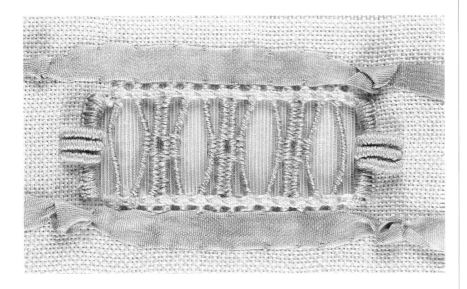

Starting at A and following the proportions shown, wrap group 1 to B on the opposite side.

Take needle and thread under the stitches at the edge and bring them out between groups 2 and 3 at C and weave them together to D. Weave groups 1 and 2 together at D. Weave groups 2 and 3 together to the other side at E.

Take needle and thread under the stitches at the edge and bring them out at group 4, F. Wrap group 4 to G, weave groups 3 and 4 together at G and wrap group 4 to the other side at H.

Take needle and thread under the stitches at the edge to the next group to be worked.

Detail from the parchment greeting card (page 67), showing a wrapped and needlewoven pattern over 4 groups of 4 fabric threads

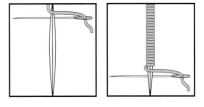

Wrapped bar worked over one group of fabric threads

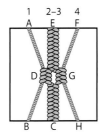

Wrapped and needlewoven pattern over 4 groups of 4 fabric threads, in a border 22 threads deep

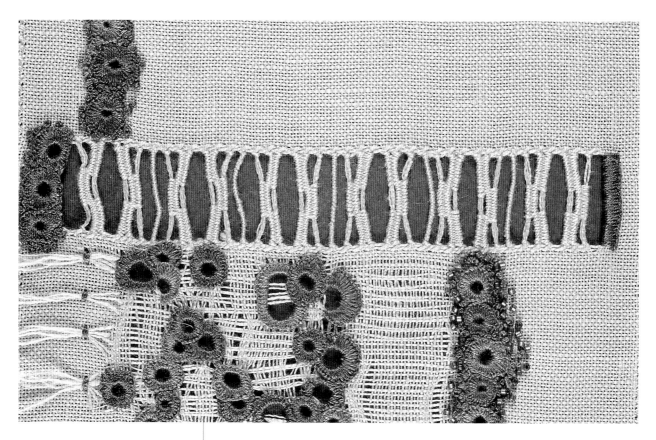

Detail from the journal cover (page 87), showing needlewoven pattern over 3 groups of 3 fabric threads; note the single wrapped bars separating the groups in the finished embroidery

Woven pattern over 3 groups of 3 fabric threads, 22 threads deep

Starting at A, weave groups 2–3 for one-third of the depth. At B weave groups 1–2 together for one-third, and then groups 2–3 again to C. The next group is worked mirror image.

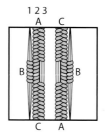

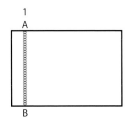

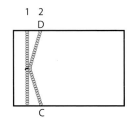

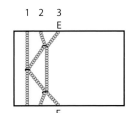

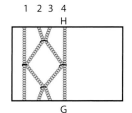

Detail of wrapped diamond pattern from serviette (page 103)

Wrapped diamond pattern over 4 groups of 4 fabric threads, 20 deep

Wrap first group, A to B. Wrap second group from C to D, making a loop around group 1 halfway. Wrap third group from E to F, making a loop around group 2 at the one-quarter and three-quarter points. Wrap fourth group from G to H, making a loop around group 3 halfway.

Horizontal woven triangles border with corner feature

Instruction with Diamond and Pearls project on page 108.

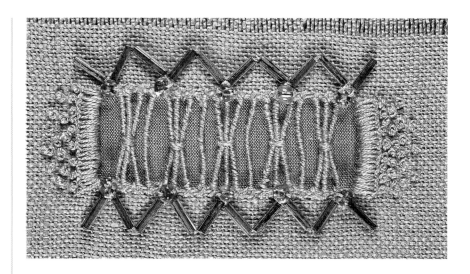

Detail from the silver blue greeting card (page 67), showing wrapped groups of threads in threes, tied together by a buttonhole stitch in the centre made while wrapping the third bar and separated by single wrapped groups

Detail from the potpourri bag (page 91) showing the decorative woven panels

Upper panel Woven blocks over 2 groups of 3 fabric threads, 22 deep. Wrap one group from A to the centre, then weave groups 1–2 to B. Weave groups 3–4 from C to the centre, and groups 2–3 to D. Continue in this manner, finishing by wrapping over one group.

Central panel Lacy woven pattern over 9 groups of 3 fabric threads, 22 threads deep.

Step 1 Weave from A to B as follows: groups 1–5 for one-quarter of the depth, groups 1–4 to halfway, 1–3 for three-quarters and 1–2 for the last quarter.

Step 2 Weave from C to D as follows: 3–4 for one-quarter of the depth, groups 4–5 to halfway, 5–6 to three-quarters, and 6–7 for the last quarter.

Step 3 Weave from E to F as follows: groups 8–9 for one-quarter of the depth, groups 7–9 to halfway, 6–9 for three-quarters and 5–9 for the last quarter.

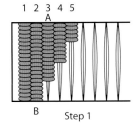

Step 1

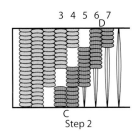

Step 2

Lower panel Woven pattern over 5 groups of 3 fabric threads, 20 deep. Starting at A, weave groups 2–3 for one-quarter of the depth, and groups 1–4 halfway. Take a loop around one or two fabric threads of each group on either side, then weave around groups 1–4 to three-quarters, and groups 2–3 for the last quarter, finishing at B.

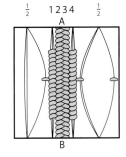

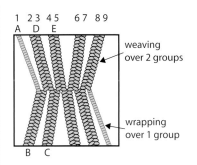

weaving over 2 groups

wrapping over 1 group

Upper panel, **woven blocks over 2 groups of 3 fabric threads**, 22 deep

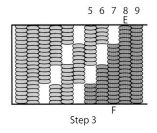

Step 3

Central panel, **lacy woven pattern over 9 groups of 3 fabric threads**, 22 threads deep

Lower panel, **woven pattern over 5 groups of 3 fabric threads**, 20 deep

Section 5
Surface stitches

GENERAL HINTS

To stab or to scoop?

There are two ways of making a stitch—scooping and stabbing. Scooping is where the needle is taken in and out of the fabric in one step and stabbing is where one movement at a time is made, that is, in then out. Except where difficulty is being experienced I recommend the stab method—there is more control of the tension and placement of stitches, as the needle enters and exits the fabric almost at a right angle and puckering of the fabric is minimised.

Looped stitches

Looped stitches such as chain and buttonhole require several steps, as shown on the diagram.

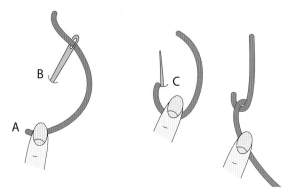

Working a looped stitch

Bring the needle up and pull it through at the starting point at A. Push the needle down at B while holding the loop in place. Push the needle from the back to the front at C.

Tension

Your tension must be sufficient to result in smooth stitches but not so great as to stretch the yarn, which causes puckering. Practice and observation will allow you to get the feel for best results. In any case don't pull the thread from the shoulder in one movement to tension a stitch. Best results are achieved when two steps are taken to tension each stitch—pull most of the thread through and pull the tension approximately 8 cm (3 in) away from the stitch. Hold the yarn with the thumb of the other hand (left for right-handers, right for left-handers) away from the stitching area while you work the next stitch. There are major benefits in using this method as the thumb acts as a stabiliser, it prevents the tension of previous stitches from being accidentally tightened, and the view of the stitching area is clear.

Tension the stitch by pulling the thread level with the fabric to prevent the looped edge rolling. Hold it in place while the next stitch is made.

Starting a new thread midstream

To start a new thread when working looped stitches such as chain and buttonhole, the use of two needles is recommended. When the working thread has almost run out, pull the last stitch to the correct tension and park the thread to one side, A in diagram. Bring a second needle and thread out through the loop of the last stitch made by the first thread, B in diagram. Work stitches with the new thread, C. Take the old needle and thread to the back through the same hole at B and secure it.

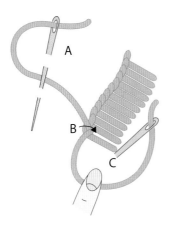

Starting a new thread midstream

STITCH GLOSSARY

Bullion stitch

Use milliners/straw needles, size 1 for 6 strands, size 3 for 3 or 4 strands, size 5 or size 7 for 1 or 2 strands.

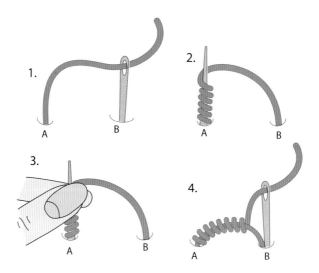

Bullion stitch

1   Bring needle and thread out at A, down into B

2   Bring the needle almost out at A. Hold it at the back with right hand (opposite for left-handers). Loosely wrap thread clockwise around needle. First wrap 3 times and push wraps towards the fabric so that the first one sits on the surface (this prevents a loop showing at the end). Continue wrapping the desired number of times, pausing every 4–6 wraps to adjust the tension, stroking clockwise to tighten, anti-clockwise to loosen. Loosen the tension of the last 2 or 3 wraps slightly to prevent making a tight wrap at the top, which will cause a point at the end of the bullion.

3   Hold wraps until all the thread is pulled through.

4   Finish into B.

Chain and whipped chain stitch

1   Chain stitch/lazy daisy (detached chain)

2   Continuous chain stitch line

3   Whipped chain—whip one stitch around each stitch in a line of chain stitch between the chain stitch and the top of the fabric.

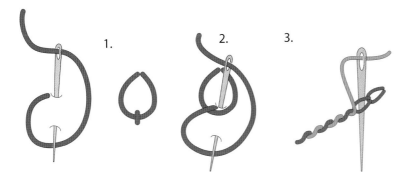

Chain and whipped chain stitch

Buttonhole eyelets

Buttonhole stitches are worked with firm tension down into the centre hole of an eyelet in a square, circle, oval or organic shape. Start by making two circles of running stitches around the centre hole and enlarge the hole by gently rotating an awl or the tips of the closed blades of your embroidery scissors in it. Tuck the last buttonhole stitch under the first. For a double buttonhole eyelet work a second layer of shorter stitches over the first layer, as shown in the diagram.

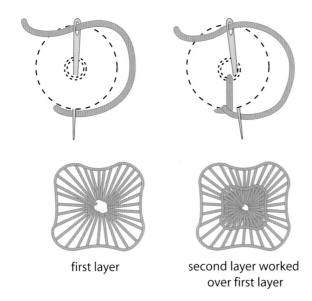

first layer   second layer worked over first layer

Buttonhole eyelet and double buttonhole eyelet

Eyelet stitch

Plain eyelets are worked in the same way as buttonhole eyelets into a centre hole, making straight stitches with firm tension.

Straight stitch eyelet

Buttonhole shading

Outline the edge of the shape to be filled with back stitch. Work buttonhole stitches approximately 5–6 mm (½ in) long close together along the outline, with the loops covering the back stitch. Add another row, overlapping the first row by 1–2 mm (¹⁄₁₀ in), A. Continue working rows until the shape is filled. Where unwanted gaps appear between the stitches, add straight stitches to fill them.

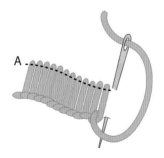
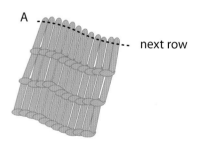

next row

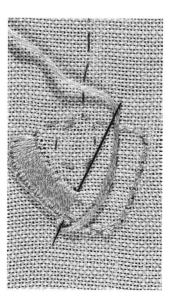
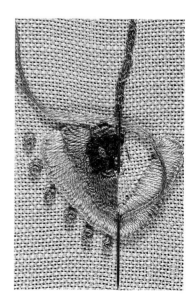

Buttonhole shading

French knot

1 Bring needle out at A. Hold yarn with the thumb and first finger and rest the needle on top of the yarn.

2 Wrap a loop towards you around the needle, B.

3 Twist the needle sideways and towards you, C, and insert into the fabric a short distance away from A.

4 Adjust the required tension and pull through, D.

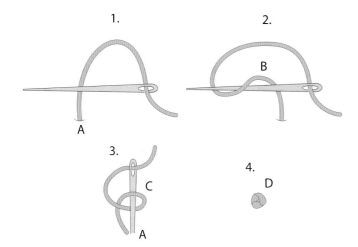

French knot

Raised chain band

This stitch is worked in two movements over a group of fabric threads using perle 5 or silk ribbon in a tapestry needle. Turn the embroidery so that you are working *down* the border, rather than across it.

1 Beginning in the buttonholed short edge of the border, bring needle and thread or ribbon out just above the centre of the first group of fabric threads. Push needle south to north, under and to the left-hand side of the bar.

Raised chain band

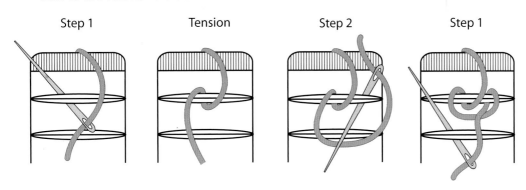

Step 1   Tension   Step 2   Step 1

2   Shows step 1 completed after pulling the thread firmly to tension.

3   Form a loop and push the needle, north to south, under the right-hand side of the bar with the loop under the needle. Pull tension lightly with thread or ribbon parallel to the fabric.

4   The final tension is created by step 1 of the next raised chain, as shown in 2 above.

Woven picot

1   Insert a pin into the fabric, A-B, which determines the length of the picot. With perle 8 in a size 24 tapestry needle bring thread out at C, 3 mm (⅛ in) to the left of B, and take it behind the pin-head, not through the fabric (ntf), and insert into D, 3 mm (⅛ in) to the right of B.

2   Bring the needle out at B. Take the thread behind the pin-head again and tighten the tension.

3   Starting at the pin-head, weave the first row under, over and under the three foundation threads, making the first few stitches very firm, and pushing the rows close together as you weave. Do not take the needle through the fabric.

4   When you get to the base of the foundation threads, finish the thread at the back and remove the pin to produce a free-standing picot, E, which may be twisted and secured into position with a stitch through the point, F. It may also be rolled to form a rose, G, which needs to be secured several times around the base. Both forms are used in the detail shown here from the diamond and pearls bag (page 107).

Twisted and rolled woven picots

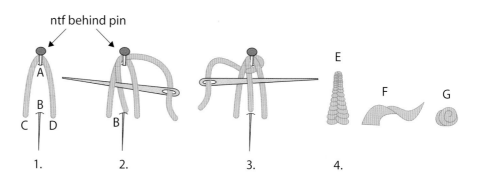

Woven picot

Section 6
Finishing

TASSELS

1 Cut a template out of heavy card, 3 cm (1¼ in) square. Wind 80 wraps of perle 8 around the template, narrower at the top and fanning out at the bottom, A.

Add the tying cord, 60 cm (24 in) of perle 8 thread, doubled, in a tapestry needle, by inserting it between the wrapped thread and the card at the top or narrow end of the tassel, B. Remove the needle.

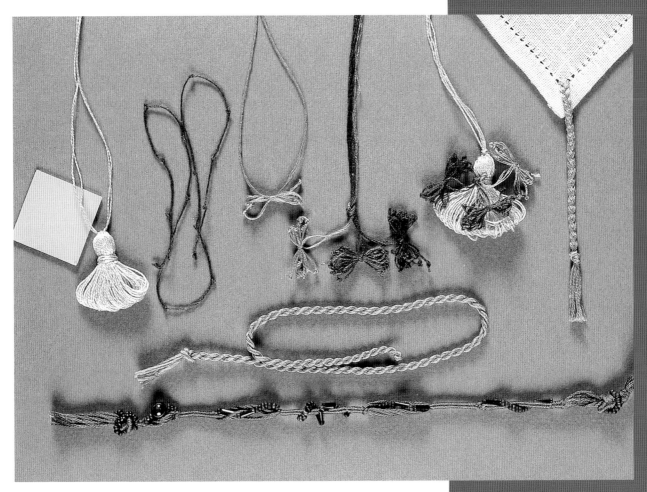

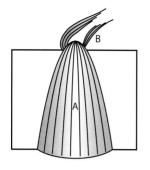

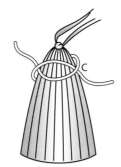

Making a tassel

2 Tie two knots in the tying cord. Remove the tassel from the card. Tie the neck with 30 cm (12 in) of thread as follows: lay the thread on a table or your knee and place the tassel on top. Tie the neck, approximately 1 cm (⅜ in) once below the top, C, and turn the tassel over. Tie another two knots.

3 Wrap the remaining ends three times around the neck, thread them into a tapestry needle and take them into the body of the tassel just above the neck and through into the skirt, D. Trim the ends. The skirt of the tassel may now be cut and trimmed. Add strings of knots stitched to the neck for a more decorative effect.

String of knots

1 Cut 50 cm (½ yd) of 3 strands cotton. Tie two knots on top of each other approximately every 2.5 cm (1 in).

2 Fold the knotted thread in a zigzag fashion to create a bunch with the knots at each side.

3 Lay a 27 cm (¾ yd) length of 3 strands cotton on a table or your knee, tie and knot it twice around the middle of the bunch. Thread the ends through a tapestry needle and attach them to the neck of a tassel.

String of knots

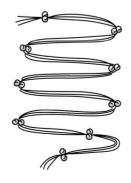

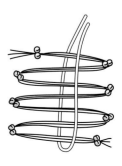

Knotted tassel

Tie three or more strings of knots together with a knot.

PLAITED FRINGE

1   Thread 3 x 33 cm (14 in) lengths of 6 strands cotton into a tapestry needle. Take the needle and threads through one hole in the antique hem stitch edge of a border and out the next, pulling them through. Remove the needle and adjust the ends of the thread until they are all even and divide them into 3 groups of 2 lengths.

2   Plait them together for approximately 8 cm (3 in) and tie them all together in a knot. Secure the knot by stitching it with one strand of matching thread and trim the ends 12 mm (1 in) below the knot.

TWISTED CORD

The length of thread required to make a twisted cord is approximately four to six times the length of the finished cord. Multiply the number of lengths depending on the thickness of the cord. For example 2 lengths of 6 strands cotton 2 m (2 yd) long results in a twisted cord approximately 75 cm (30 in) long.

By hand

Step1 Double the yarn around a hook and twist all the strands until tightly coiled.

Step2 Holding the end in one hand, double the coiled yarn and hold it taut with the index finger of the other hand at the halfway point. Rotate your index finger to start the cord twisting along its length, removing your finger while still holding the two ends together with the other hand.

Step3 Let it twist back on itself and knot the ends.

By machine

Attach yarn through a hole in the bobbin and twist as above.

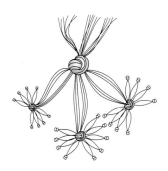

Knotted tassel

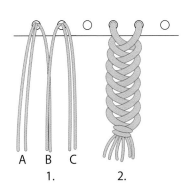

Plaited fringe

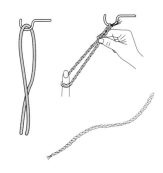

Twisting a cord by hand

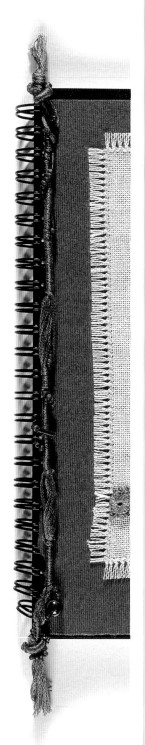

WRAPPED AND BEADED CORD

Beads are incorporated in a wrapped cord in two ways—laying them beside a section of unwrapped threads or over a wrapped section.

1   Make a 'bead string' as follows: thread 2 m (2 yd) beading thread or waxed cotton into a beading or size 10 crewel needle and double it, tying a small bead on the end to stop the beads from falling off (stopper bead). Thread your choice of beads onto the bead string for 20 cm (8 in). Place the end of the needle into a cork.

2   Cut 8 x 1 m (1 yd) lengths of 6-stranded cotton and tie them and the bead string together with a knot. Attach the knotted end with masking tape to the edge of a table.

3   Separate one length of cotton (6 strands) and wrap it around all the other threads, including the string holding the beads (the core), for approximately 2–4 cm (¾–1½ in), A. Tie off the thread with a half-hitch knot (like a buttonhole stitch), B.

(**Note**   Right-handers wrap clockwise and left-handers anti-clockwise. Hold cord firmly as you wrap. To take a break in the middle of wrapping simply 'park' by tying a loose half-hitch. When ready to resume undo it and continue wrapping.)

Separate a number of beads, C, and tie another half-hitch knot around the core, below the beads, D.

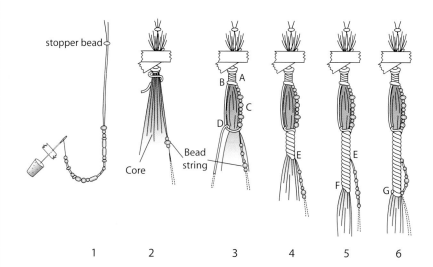

Wrapped and beaded cord

4   Separate another length of cotton (6 strands), wrap it around the core for approximately 2 cm (¾ in) and tie with a half-hitch knot at E.

5   Separate the bead string from the core at E, and continue wrapping the thread around the core for another 2 cm (¾ in) to F and tie off with a half-hitch knot.

6   Push beads into place up the string and tie another half-hitch knot around all the threads and the bead string, G.

Continue wrapping and incorporating beads to make the length of cord required.

To extend the length bring in 1 m (1 yd) lengths of thread by including them in the wrapping. To add more beads stitch the remaining thread of the bead string into the core and attach another bead string.

BUTTONHOLE BARS AND LOOPS

Buttonhole bars are used as channels for threading ribbon or cords as drawstrings. Using perle 8 make two straight stitches approximately 6 mm (½ in) long in the same holes, A-B, and buttonhole stitch them, C.

Buttonhole loops are made in the same way except that the two foundation stitches are longer and the first buttonhole stitch is pulled tight so that the loops don't slip. They are used as a fastener around a button.

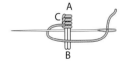

Buttonhole bar or loop

61

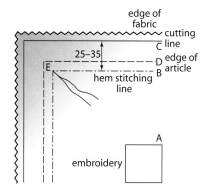

Preparing a hem

HEMS

Preparing the edge

There are two ways to prepare the edges of an article for hemming. In method 1 fabric threads are counted evenly on all sides, outwards from the open work borders. In method 2 counting starts from the edge of the fabric inwards. Both methods are illustrated by the diagram.

Method 1 Counting from the open work border towards the edge

On all sides count the desired number of fabric threads from A, the edge of the embroidery, to B, the hem-stitching line, and mark B with a pin. Cut and withdraw the next fabric thread in the centre of each side and pull them back to meet at the corners.

On all sides count 25 to 35 fabric threads from B to C, the cutting line, and mark with a pin. Withdraw the next fabric thread. Line D is approximately one-third of the distance away from the hem-stitching line and marks the edge of the article. Its position varies by one or two fabric threads depending on where the first fold of the hem is made. A thread is not withdrawn on this line. Turn the hem as described below.

Method 2 Counting from the edge of the fabric

Pull out a fabric thread close to the edge of the fabric, C. This is the cutting line. Count 25 to 35 fabric threads towards the centre of the article, from C to B, and mark with a pin. Cut and withdraw the next fabric thread in the centre of each side and pull them back to meet at the corners. This is the hem-stitching line, B. Turn the hem as described below.

Tails of withdrawn threads at the corners are tucked into the hems at E, or pull out one tail in the corner and weave the remaining one in the space.

Cutting and turning the hem

1   Cut on the cutting line to remove excess fabric.

2   Fold the edges of two opposite sides, a few fabric threads less than one-third of the width of the hem, for example, 7 or eight 8 threads for a hem 25 fabric threads wide or 10 or 11 fabric threads for a hem 35 fabric threads wide. Finger-press from the centre out to the corners. Before folding the hem again, 'shave' off a small amount of fabric at the corners to flatten them.

3   Fold the hem again so that the folded edge made previously almost meets the hem-stitching line. Pin the hem and tack it in place with sewing cotton. This fold positions line D, the edge of the finished article.

4   Repeat steps 2 and 3 on the other sides.

Note Narrow hems like these cannot be mitred as most embroidery fabrics available today fray easily, being manufactured for the cross-stitch market with large spaces between the threads, easily seen and penetrated. The hems in this book are based on traditional narrow European hems, which were folded at the corners.

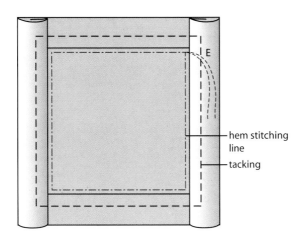

Cutting and turning hem

Antique hem stitch

Holding the edge of the hem towards you, work antique hem stitch using perle 8 or 2 strands cotton in a size 24 tapestry needle, following the diagram. This stitch may be worked holding the fabric horizontally or vertically. This is the same stitch as the one used to divide fabric threads into groups, the difference being that here it is worked between the folded edge of the hem and the hem-stitching line. Start the thread through the edge of the hem at A, using a waste knot, and bring it out at B, two fabric threads below the fold, and work as follows:

Step 1 Holding the stitching thread towards you, make one stitch into the hem-stitching line, picking up four fabric threads, C-D.

Step 2 Holding the stitching thread away from you, take the needle out through the fold of the hem with firm tension, inserting the needle from the back to the front at E, two fabric threads below the fold and opposite C.

Repeat until the corner is reached where the last stitch may be made over 2, 3 or 5 fabric threads as necessary. Make an extra stitch in the corner to secure it.

Thread a crewel needle with matching sewing cotton and stitch through the fabric at the corners to hold them in place.

Working antique hem stitch

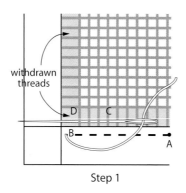

Step 1

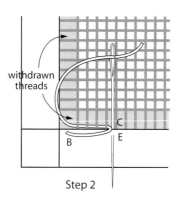

Step 2

Ladder stitch

Worked with matching sewing cotton in an embroidery needle, ladder stitch is ideal for joining two edges together without the stitches showing. The needle enters the fold of the fabric exactly opposite making vertical stitches B–C, D–E, etc.

Working ladder stitch

KNOTTED BUTTONHOLE INSERTION

This stitch can be used to make a decorative join between two finished edges. It is used to join the back and front of the roses drawstring purse (page 73).

Steps 1 and 2 Work buttonhole stitches approximately 6 mm (¼ in) wide on the two edges to be joined.

Steps 3 and 4 Hold the two buttonholed edges together, right sides facing out, and wrap twice over and through each loop. The loops may not always be opposite each other and may be whipped once or twice as their relative positions indicate.

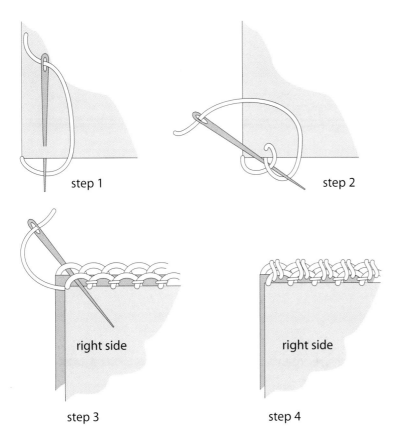

step 1

step 2

right side

right side

step 3

step 4

Knotted buttonhole insertion

65

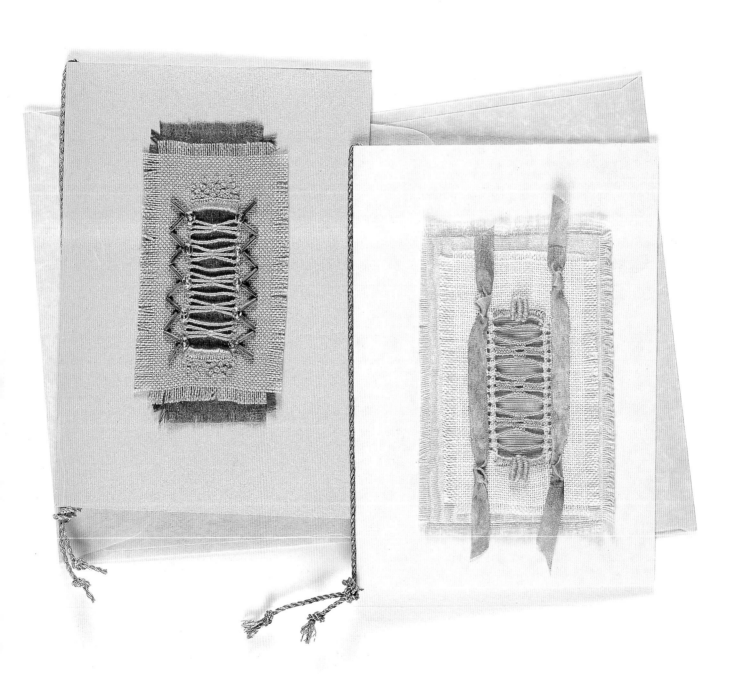

Section 7
Projects

GREETING CARDS

Greeting cards are an excellent way to sample open work patterns and stitches. These two designs may be used for other projects as well, such as bookmarks, small pouches and bags, book covers, the corners of serviettes, and coasters. These small embroideries, with a background of silk, may be stitched to items made in other fabrics or to ready-made bags, cushions and so on.

MATERIALS

12 x 8 cm (4¾ x 3¼ in) (each card) Belfast or other even weave linen, 32 count, colours 222 cream and 718 silver grey

Strips of plain fabric 10 cm (4 in) wide or as needed to fit hoop

DMC stranded cotton, 1 skein each:
> *3752 silver blue*
> *3046 yellow beige*
> *676 old gold light*
> *677 old gold very light*

1 m (1 yd) silk embroidery ribbon, 4–6 mm (⅛–¼ in) wide

Cards with envelopes or coloured card to make them (art supplier)

Ribbon or cord to decorate card

20 bugle beads and 5 round beads

Needles:
> *embroidery needle size 5 or 7*
> *milliners needle size 3*
> *tapestry needle size 24*

Embroidery hoop

Finished size of embroidery approximately 9 x 5.5 cm (3½ x 2⅛ in)

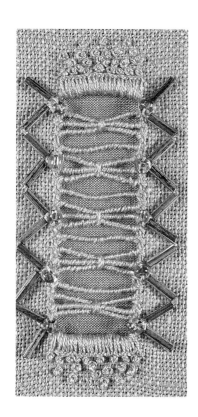

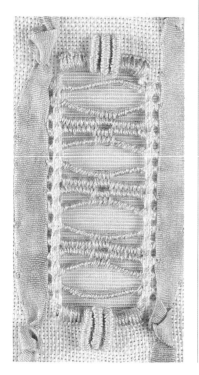

INSTRUCTIONS

Attach strips of plain fabric to the sides of the linen for use with the hoop.

SILVER BLUE COLOURWAY

Border of open work In the centre of the silver grey fabric make a border 57 fabric threads wide and 22 deep. Divide the fabric threads into 19 groups of 3 with antique hem stitch using 2 strands colour 3752.

Woven pattern Worked with 3 strands colour 3752. Three wrapped groups of fabric threads are tied in the centre with a buttonhole stitch made while the third group is being wrapped. Each tied group is separated by one wrapped group.

Secure short edges with buttonhole stitch using 3 strands 3752.

Embroidery Scatter French knots using 3 strands 3752 along the short edges. Add beads next to the border.

PARCHMENT COLOURWAY

Border of open work In the centre of the fabric make a border 56 fabric threads wide and 22 deep. Divide the fabric threads into 14 groups of 4 with four-sided stitch, using 3 strands 3046.

Woven pattern One wrapped group at the beginning and end, and three wrapped and woven patterns over 5 groups using 3 strands colour 3046.

Secure short edges with buttonhole stitch in colour 3046.

Embroidery Three bullion stitches, colour 676, 18 wraps around size 3 milliners needle, in the centre of the buttonhole stitch edges.

Cut two 15 cm (6 in) lengths of silk ribbon and tie a knot 12 mm (1 in) from each end. Stitch them either side of the border with 1 strand 3046.

MAKING UP

Trim fabric to the finished size and fringe the edge. Stitch it to coloured paper or silk fabric and glue or stitch them to a card. Add a cord or ribbon around the fold of the card.

BOOKMARKS

Like greeting cards, bookmarks are ideal projects for learning and useful articles. These designs also can be applied to greeting cards and other small projects.

MATERIALS

22.5 x 12 cm (8⅞ x 4¾ in) Belfast or other even weave linen, 32 count, colour 222 cream or 233 antique ivory

4 strips of plain fabric 5 cm (2 in) wide

1 ball DMC perle 8, colour ecru or 739 cream

Tapestry needle size 24

Embroidery hoop

Finished size approximately 21 x 6 cm (8¼ x 2⅜ in)

INSTRUCTIONS

Preparation Attach plain fabric to the sides of the linen for use with the hoop.

Pin-mark the centre of the narrow width, A. Count 26 vertical threads on either side of A, a total of 52, and withdraw the next vertical thread on both sides (hem-stitching lines), to create the centre of the bookmark.

Count 36 vertical fabric threads out from the hem-stitching lines and withdraw the next fabric thread (cutting lines). The space between the hem-stitching line and cutting line is the hem allowance.

Mark the beginning of the fringe area by withdrawing a horizontal fabric thread 3.5 cm (1½ in) in from the top and bottom of the fabric, B-C, D-E. Count 3 fabric threads inwards from these lines and withdraw the 4th, cutting in the middle and withdrawing them to the hem-stitching lines, F-G, H-I. Work a row of four-sided stitch between these lines.

Mark the end of the fringe area and the cutting lines by withdrawing the 31st horizontal thread away from B-C and D-E.

The bookmark is now ready for open work and embroidery. The hems and fringe are made after stitching is complete (see page 62).

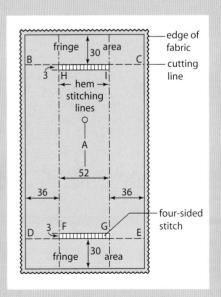

Bookmark plan

EMBELLISHMENT OF BOOKMARKS

MATERIALS

1 bookmark as above

1 skein DMC perle 5 colour ecru or 739 cream for woven bars and woven triangle bookmarks

DMC stranded cotton, 1 skein each:

ecru or 739 cream

colours of your choice for buttonhole triangles and shaded buttonhole bookmarks

Silk ribbon 4 mm (⅛ in) wide in plain or space-dyed colours, or perle 5 or 8, for raised chain band bookmark

BOOKMARK WITH WOVEN BARS

Eight horizontal fabric threads above the four-sided stitch at one end, make a border of open work 20 fabric threads deep and 40 wide edged with satin stitch using perle 5. Work 5 woven bars, each bar made around 8 fabric threads with perle 8. Secure the short edges with buttonhole stitch. Make hems and pull threads out to create fringes.

BOOKMARK WITH WOVEN TRIANGLE

Eight fabric threads above four-sided stitch at one end, make a border of open work 20 fabric threads deep and 39 wide, edged with antique hem stitch dividing the fabric threads into 13 groups of 3 with perle 8. Work a woven triangle with perle 5. Secure the short edges with buttonhole stitch. Make hems, pull threads out to create fringes, and add a tassel if desired.

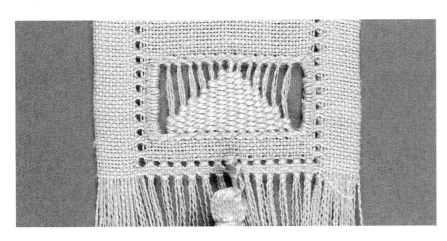

Top left, raised chain band with silk ribbon; top right, woven bars over 2 groups; lower left, woven triangle; centre, shaded buttonhole; lower right, buttonhole triangles

BOOKMARK WITH RAISED CHAIN BAND

Make a border following the instructions immediately above (for bookmark with woven triangle) and decorate the groups of fabric threads with raised chain band worked in silk ribbon, perle 5 or 8.

BOOKMARK WITH BUTTONHOLE TRIANGLES

Eight horizontal fabric threads above four-sided stitch at one end of the bookmark, make a border of open work 12 fabric threads deep and 36 wide, edged with antique hem stitch dividing the fabric threads into 18 groups of 2 with perle 8. Work three buttonhole-stitched triangles in the colour of your choice. Secure the short edges with buttonhole stitch.

BOOKMARK WITH SHADED BUTTONHOLE

Work a line of antique hem stitch 2 cm (¾ in) above the line of four-sided stitch and fill the space with shaded buttonhole shapes in colours of your choice. Add strings of knots.

HEMS AND FRINGE

Cut on the cutting lines to trim excess fabric.

Fold 8 fabric threads in from the edge, and finger-press.

Fold again so that the first fold meets the hem-stitching line and tack in place.

Stitch antique hem stitch with perle 8 between the ends of four-sided stitch and press. Remove the fabric threads at each end to create fringes.

ROSES
DRAWSTRING PURSE

Inspired by Art Nouveau roses, this project demonstrates the use of knotted buttonhole insertion to join hemmed fabric together with lacy seams.

MATERIALS

2 x 36 x 28 cm (14¼ x 11 in) Belfast linen, 32 count, colour 222 cream

Strips of plain fabric 5 cm (2 in) wide

DMC stranded cotton, 1 skein each:

> *316 antique mauve medium*
> *372 mustard light*
> *523 fern green light*
> *778 antique mauve very light*
> *3046 yellow beige medium*

1 m (1 yd) silk ribbon 4–8 mm (³⁄₁₆–⁵⁄₁₆ in) wide in plain or space-dyed colours

Needles:

> *tapestry needle size 24*
> *embroidery or crewel needle size 5 or 7*
> *milliners needle size 3*

Embroidery hoop

2 pieces lining fabric 29 x 20 cm (11½ x 8 in)

Cord or ribbon for drawstring

Finished size 27 x 18 cm (10¾ x 7 in)

INSTRUCTIONS

Attach strips of plain fabric to the sides of the linen for use with hoop.

Tack-mark a rectangle 27 x 18 cm (10¾ x 7 in) in the centre of the fabric. This is the approximate edge of the article.

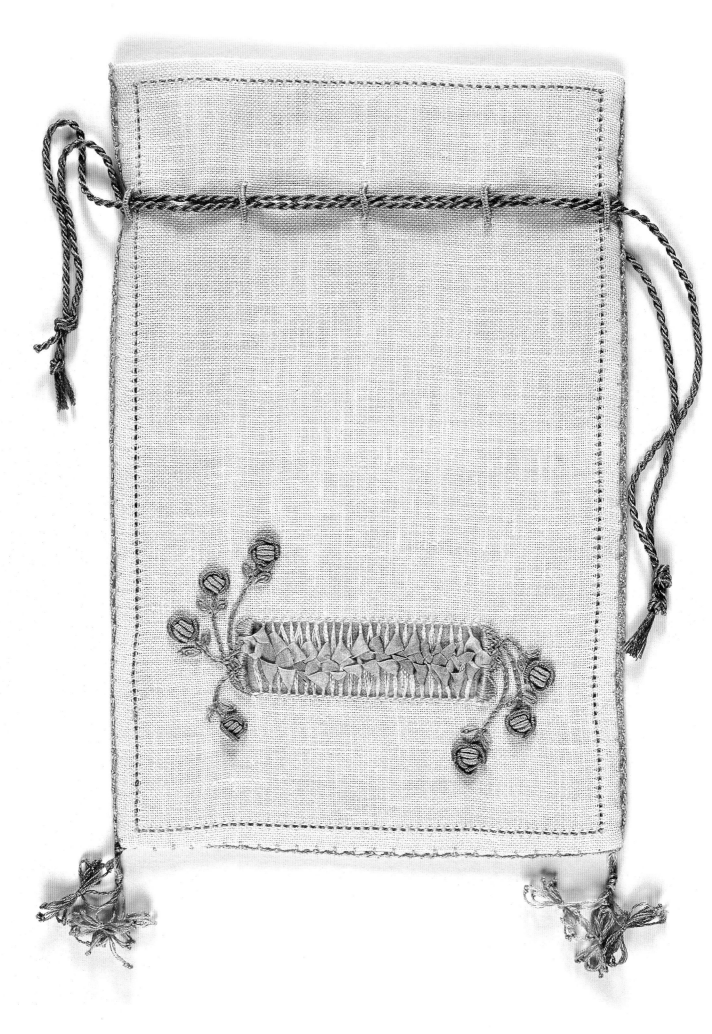

Tracing pattern for embroidery

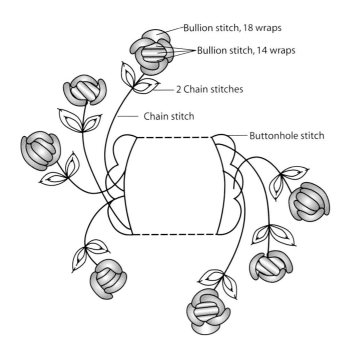

Bullion stitch, 18 wraps

Bullion stitch, 14 wraps

2 Chain stitches

Chain stitch

Buttonhole stitch

Border of open work Commencing 5.5 cm (2¼ in) above the tack-mark on the narrow edge of the article, make a border of open work 96 fabric threads wide and 30 deep, divided into 24 groups of 4 with antique hem stitch using 3 strands colour 3046.

Secure short edges of border with three scallops of buttonhole stitch using 3 strands 3046.

Raised chain band, using the silk ribbon in a tapestry needle, is worked through the groups of fabric threads, commencing and finishing through the buttonhole stitch edges.

Embroidery Trace the stems of the roses onto the fabric and work them with chain stitch using 3 strands 523. Leaves are two chain stitches over each other in colour 372. Roses are made with 3 strands cotton in a size 3 milliners needle as follows: three bullion stitches side by side form the centre of each rose, 14 wraps around the needle in 778. The large roses have 5 and the small roses 3 bullion stitches placed diagonally around the central three, 18 wraps around the needle in 316.

Hem Cut and withdraw one fabric thread 9 fabric threads in from the tack-marked edge of the article to create the hem-stitching line.

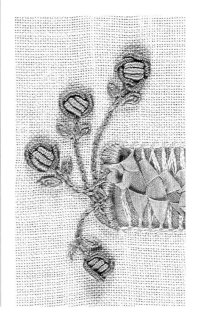

Cut and withdraw another fabric thread 25 fabric threads out from the hem-stitching line towards the edge. This is the cutting line.

Cut on the cutting line to trim excess fabric.

Turn the hem and stitch with antique hem stitch using 3 strands colour 3046.

Make five buttonhole bars, 4 cm (1½ in) below the top of the bag, on both front and back, in the positions shown in the photograph.

The back of the bag is the same as the front, but is worked without the open work panel or the embroidery.

Lining The front and back of the bag are lined separately. Press the edges of the lining pieces over so that they meet the hem-stitching lines. Pin the lining to the back of the fabric and stitch it to the hem-stitching line.

Join the front and the back with knotted buttonhole insertion or ladder stitch.

Drawstring Thread two cords (colour 316) or ribbons 50 cm (½ yd) long through the buttonhole bars, one cord or ribbon entering and exiting on one side, the other entering and exiting on the other side. Knot the ends together.

Knotted tassels Attach knotted tassels in colours 316, 778 and 372 to the bottom corners.

SAMPLER PANEL

This sampler panel incorporates many of the techniques featured in this book—use similar colours or substitute your own.

MATERIALS

30 x 25 cm (12 x 10 in) Cashel linen, 28 count, colour 222 cream

Strips of plain fabric 5 cm (2 in) wide (if using a hoop)

DMC stranded cotton, 1 skein each:

> ecru
> 503 blue green medium
> 676 old gold light
> 783 topaz medium
> 926 grey green medium
> 927 grey green light
> 928 grey green very light
> 3768 grey green dark

DMC perle 5, 1 skein ecru

DMC perle 8, 1 ball ecru

Needles:

> tapestry needle size 24
> embroidery or crewel needle size 5 or 7

Embroidery frame (preferable) or hoop

Finished size 30 x 25 cm (12 x 10 in); mounted in 25 x 20 cm (10 x 8 in) frame with 17 x 11.5 cm (6¾ x 4½ in) opening

INSTRUCTIONS

Lace fabric to the embroidery frame or attach plain fabric to the sides of linen for use with the hoop.

Borders All borders are stitched with perle 8 ecru. All edges are buttonhole stitched with 3 strands ecru. All embroidery stitches are worked in 3 strands cotton.

Row 1 Buttonhole triangles. Border 12 fabric threads deep and 90 wide divided into 30 groups of 3 fabric threads with antique hem stitch; buttonhole triangles using 6 strands cotton in size 24 tapestry needle are each worked over 6 groups.

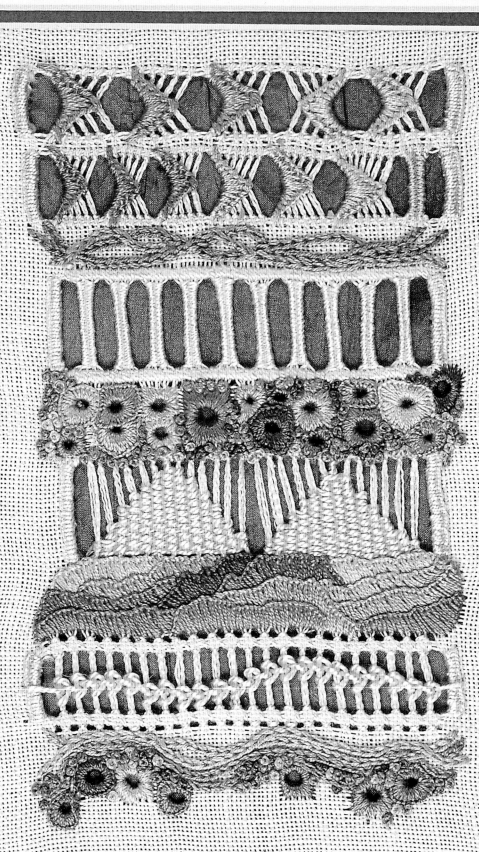

Row 2 Buttonhole triangles and woven bar. Leave 5 fabric threads and open a border 12 fabric threads deep and 88 wide divided into 44 groups of 2 with antique hem stitch. Work 3 buttonhole triangles over 6 groups of fabric threads, 2 over 7 groups, one over 8 groups, and a woven bar over the last 4 groups, all with 6 strands cotton.

Row 3 Woven bars. Leave 10 fabric threads and open a border 20 deep and 80 wide edged with satin stitch and stitch woven bars over 2 groups of 4 fabric threads using perle 8 ecru. Between rows 2 and 3 work three lines of chain stitch.

Row 4 Woven triangles. Leave 15 fabric threads and open a border 22 deep and 78 wide divided into 26 groups of 3 with antique hem stitch, and stitch woven triangles over 13 groups with perle 5 ecru. Between rows 3 and 4 work a random arrangement of buttonhole eyelets, eyelets and French knots.

Row 5 Raised chain band. Leave 15 fabric threads and open a border 15 deep and 88 wide divided into groups of 4 with four-sided stitch; work raised chain band in perle 5 ecru across the border. Between rows 4 and 5 work a pattern in shaded buttonhole. Below row 5 work chain stitch lines, buttonhole eyelets, eyelets and French knots.

FRAMING

The finished work may be custom framed or mounted in a ready-made frame without the glass. The measurements for the frame and the opening given in the materials list are standard for frames sold with glass.

To the back panel of the frame, glue a piece of plain fabric the same size, only at the corners, and a piece of coloured fabric over that. Pin the embroidery in position on top, fold the edges to the back and lace with perle 8. Remove the pins. Fold and stitch the corners, place a piece of black card over the back, and insert the sampler into the frame.

Sampler panel
Row 1: 12 deep, 90 wide, 30 groups of 3
Row 2: 12 deep, 88 wide, 44 groups of 2
Row 3: 20 deep, 80 wide
Row 4: 22 deep, 78 wide, 26 groups of 3
Row 5: 15 deep, 88 wide, 22 groups of 4

HARLEQUIN POUCH

T his useful little pouch features a multi-coloured needlewoven channel to gather the top closed with ribbons or cords.

MATERIALS

30 cm (12 in) square Belfast linen, 32 count, colour 222 cream or 233 antique ivory

Strips of plain fabric 5 cm (2 in) wide

DMC stranded cotton, 1 skein each:
> *333 blue violet very dark*
> *553 violet*
> *733 olive green*
> *921 copper*
> *3765 peacock blue dark*
> *3810 peacock blue light*
> *3827 yellow gold light*
> *3854 yellow gold medium*

Needles:
> *tapestry needle size 24*
> *embroidery or crewel needle size 5 or 7*

Embroidery hoop

1 m (1 yd) silk ribbon 6 mm (¼ in) wide to match one of the threads

Lining fabric 24 cm (9½ in) square

Finished size 21 cm (8¼ in) square, folding to 21 x 10.5 cm (8¼ x 4⅛ in)

INSTRUCTIONS

Attach strips of plain fabric to the sides of the linen for use with hoop.

Tack-mark a 21 cm (8¼ in) square in the centre of the fabric. This is the edge of the pouch.

Border of open work Commencing 4 cm (1½ in) below the top edge of the pouch, withdraw a border of 15 horizontal threads across the width of the fabric, including the seam allowance.

Separate the vertical fabric threads into groups of 3 with antique hem stitch, using 2 strands 3827, starting 12 mm (½ in) before and finishing 12 mm (½ in) over the tack-marked edges to include the seam allowance.

Woven border Commencing at the first group of vertical fabric threads on the left-hand side, weave bars worked with 3 strands cotton in a tapestry needle, as follows: *colour 3827 over 5 groups; colour 3854 over 2 groups; colour 921 over 3 groups; colour 733 over 4 groups; colour 3765 over 4 groups; colour 3746 over 5 groups; colour 333 over 4 groups and colour 553 over 3 groups.* Repeat the pattern *—* right across the border.

Embroidery Tack-mark a 7 x 3 cm (2¾ x 1⅛ in) outline for the design in the centre of the fabric, 7 cm (2¾ in) below the woven border. Work French knots and buttonhole eyelets in bands of colour blending into each other.

Making up Withdraw a fabric thread on all sides 12 mm (½ in) outside the tack-marked edge of the bag to mark the cutting line. Cut off excess fabric and overlock or zigzag stitch the edge.

Fold the fabric lengthwise, right side to the inside, pin and tack the edges and stitch them together by machine or hand.

Press the seam allowance open and flatten the bag so that the seam is at the centre back.

Stitch a seam across the base of the bag. Turn right side out and press.

Fold the top edge once and slip stitch.

Lining Machine stitch sides and base of lining, fold the top edges over and stitch close to the top edge of the bag.

Drawstring Make a channel under the woven border by run-stitching through the bag and the lining on both sides of the woven border with 3 strands colour 3827. Thread two ribbons 50 cm (½ yd) long through the channel, one ribbon entering and exiting on one side, and the other entering and exiting on the other side. Knot the ends together.

Knotted tassels Attach four knotted tassels in colours 333, 553, 3827 and 3854 to the base of the embroidery.

PEARL PURSE

A wrapped and beaded cord strung with pearls adds complementary texture to the needlewoven border embellished with smooth shiny pearls and bullion stitches.

MATERIALS

*40 x 28 cm (16 x 11 in) Belfast linen, 32 count, colour 222 cream
or 233 antique ivory*

1 ball DMC perle 8, colour ecru or 739 cream

*2 skeins DMC stranded cotton, colour ecru or 739 cream
(1 for cord)*

Needles:

> *tapestry needle size 24*
> *embroidery or crewel needle size 5or 7*
> *beading needle or embroidery needle size 10*
> *milliners/straw needle size 3*

Sewing cotton, cream colour and beeswax or beading thread

Embroidery hoop

13 pearls 5 mm (¼ in) diameter for embroidery

Assorted pearls and dress beads for wrapped and beaded cord

Lining fabric 35 x 20 cm (13¾ x 8 in)

Finished size 32 x 17 cm (12⅝ x 6¾ in), folding to 17 x 12 cm (6¾ x 4¾ in)

INSTRUCTIONS

Tack-mark a rectangle 32 x 17 cm (12⅝ x 6¾ in) in the centre of the fabric. This is the finished size of the purse.

Border of open work Commencing 2 cm (¾ in) above the tack-mark of one narrow end of the fabric, make a border of open work 123 fabric threads wide and 22 deep, divided into 41 groups of 3 with antique hem stitch using perle 8.

Woven border Work a woven pattern over 9 groups, beginning, alternating and ending with single whipped bars, using perle 8 in a tapestry needle.

Secure short edges of border with buttonhole stitch using 3 strands ecru or 739.

Pearls Guided by the photo, attach 10 pearls above the border with beading thread or sewing cotton pulled through beeswax, twice through each pearl. Attach a pearl at each short edge.

Embroidery Bullion stitches using 4 strands in ecru or 739, wrapped 18 times around a number 3 milliners needle. Work the pairs of vertical stitches between the pearls first, then two curved ones around each pearl, beginning at the base and ending halfway up the vertical bullion stitches.

Hem Cut and withdraw one fabric thread 11 fabric threads in from the tack-marked edges to create the hem-stitching line. Cut and withdraw another fabric thread 32 fabric threads out from the hem-stitching line towards the edge. This is the cutting line.

Cut on the cutting line to trim excess fabric.

Turn the hem and stitch with antique hem stitch using perle 8 colour ecru or 739.

Lining Press the edges of the lining fabric over so that the lining meets the hem-stitching line. Pin to the back of the embroidery and stitch to the hem-stitching line.

Finishing Fold up the plain end of the fabric for 9 cm (3½ in), and stitch the sides together with ladder stitch.

Attach a pearl to the middle edge of the embroidered flap, fold flap down and make a buttonhole loop below it.

Make a wrapped and beaded cord 36 cm (14 in) long, incorporating assorted pearls and dress beads onto the bead string, tie a knot at each end and attach it to the top corners of the bag.

JOURNAL OR
BOOK COVER

Buttonhole eyelets form a lovely random, lacy pattern complementing a geometric needlewoven border. The eyelets are worked on an area of fabric threads moved about with a needle after other threads have been withdrawn. Some withdrawn vertical threads are stitched together to form a fringe.

MATERIALS

25.5 x 15 cm (10 x 6 in) Belfast linen, 32 count, colour 222 cream or 233 antique ivory

1 ball DMC perle 8 colour ecru or 739 cream

DMC stranded cotton, 1 skein each:

> *3328 salmon dark*
> *3712 salmon medium*
> *2 skeins 3722 shell pink medium (1 for cord)*

Needles:

> *tapestry needle size 24*
> *beading needle or embroidery needle size 10*
> *milliners/straw needle size 3*

Sewing cotton and beeswax or beading thread to attach beads

Embroidery hoop

Assorted dress beads for wrapped and beaded cord

A5 size journal or sketch book

Finished size 17 x 11.5 cm (6¾ x 4½ in)

INSTRUCTIONS

Tack-mark a rectangle 16 x 10 cm (6¼ x 4 in) in the centre of the fabric. This indicates the inner edge of the fringe. On all sides count 10 fabric threads towards the edge of the fabric and withdraw the 11th to mark the cutting line.

Border of open work Commencing 3.5 cm (1½ in) away from the long side, make a border of open work 339 fabric threads long and 25 deep, divided into 113 groups of 3 fabric threads with antique hem stitch using perle 8.

Weaving Woven pattern over 3 groups, mirror image, separated by one wrapped group, using perle 8.

Embroidery Starting 4 cm (1½ in) below the top on the right-hand side of the border, cut and withdraw every third vertical fabric thread as far as 2.5 cm (1 in) above the lower edge. Move the remaining fabric threads into patterns with a tapestry needle and work buttonhole eyelets randomly with 3 strands of all colours. Two of the buttonhole eyelets are worked so that vertical fabric threads are incorporated to form part of their centres. Using 3 strands colour 3722, stitch the withdrawn fabric threads into groups of 4 or 5, 1 cm (⅜ in) below their exit point at the bottom of the embroidery and trim. Add small dress beads and French knots around the buttonhole eyelets as desired.

Secure the top edge of the border with buttonhole stitch in 3 strands colour 3722, and the lower edge with buttonhole eyelets and French knots in 3 strands 3722 and 3328, and work more buttonhole eyelets and French knots to the left of the border in the same colours.

Fringe Work antique hem stitch on all four sides with perle 8, holding the edge of the fabric away from you. Cut on the cutting line and remove fabric threads to form the fringe.

Finishing Stitch the embroidery onto coloured card with edges torn. To tear the card, fold it on the line to be torn and apply a little water with a sponge to the back. Place a ruler on the fold and gently tear along it. Glue the card with the embroidery to the front of the journal or sketch book.

Make a wrapped and beaded cord 28 cm (11 in) long and attach it to the journal.

POTPOURRI BAG OR GLASSES CASE

A subtle antique colour scheme of embroidery enhances three different needlewoven patterns. Delicate gold organza ribbon threaded through buttonhole bars draws the bag closed.

MATERIALS

30 cm (12 in) square Belfast linen, 32 count, colour 222 cream or 233 antique ivory

Strips of plain fabric 5 cm (2 in) wide

1 ball DMC perle 8, colour ecru or 739 cream

DMC stranded cotton, 1 skein each:

> *372 mustard*
> *783 topaz*
> *832 golden olive*
> *3012 khaki green*
> *3041 antique violet*

Needles:

> *tapestry needle size 24*
> *embroidery or crewel needle size 5 or 7*
> *milliners or straw needle size 3*

Embroidery hoop

1.5 m (1½ yd) ribbon 6 mm (¼ in) wide, or cord

Lining fabric 24 cm (9½ in) square

Finished size 21 cm (8¼ in) square, folding to 21 x 10.5 cm (8¼ x 4⅛ in)

INSTRUCTIONS

Attach plain fabric to the sides of the linen for use with the hoop.

Tack-mark a 21 cm (8¼ in) square in the centre of the fabric to indicate the edges of the finished work. Tack-mark the vertical centre of the fabric.

Borders of open work In the centre of the fabric create three borders. The lower border commences 3 cm (1¼ in) above the tack-marked bottom edge and is 93 fabric threads wide and 20 deep.

Above it leave 24 fabric threads and open the middle border, which is 93 fabric threads wide and 22 deep. Above it leave 18 fabric threads and open the top border, 87 fabric threads wide and 22 deep.

Using perle 8, divide all borders into groups of 3 fabric threads with antique hem stitch. The lower and middle borders result in 31 groups each, and the top border 29 groups.

Weaving All weaving is worked with perle 8.

Lower border Woven pattern over 5 groups of fabric threads.

Centre border Lacy woven pattern over 9 groups of fabric threads, beginning, ending and separated by one wrapped group.

Upper border Woven blocks.

Secure short edges of borders with buttonhole stitch in colour 3041, a row of chain stitch in colour 832, and French knots in colour 783, all using 3 strands.

Embroidery Follow the illustration for approximate placement of bullion stitch flowers, 4 strands wrapped 12 times around size 3 milliners needle using colours 3041 and 832. French knot centres are in 3 strands 783, the other French knots in 3 strands 3012. Work the buttonhole eyelets in 3 strands 3041, 3012 and 372.

Hem Withdraw one fabric thread 11 fabric threads in from the tack-marked edges to create the hem-stitching lines. Cut and withdraw another fabric thread 32 fabric threads out from the hem-stitching line towards the edge. This is the cutting line. Cut on the cutting line to trim excess fabric. Turn the hem and stitch with antique hem stitch using perle 8.

Lining Press the edges of the lining fabric over so that the lining meets the hem-stitching lines. Pin to the back of the embroidery and stitch to the hem-stitching line.

Finishing Fold the fabric lengthwise, right side to the inside, and pin the side hems together. Using perle 8 in a tapestry needle, stitch the sides together, 2 fabric threads in from the edge, with ladder stitch. Flatten the bag so that the seam is in the centre back, and ladder stitch the lower edge. Turn the bag to the right side and press.

Make a channel for the drawstring by working 8 buttonholed bars at the top of the bag, 3 cm (1⅛ in) down from the edge.

Thread two ribbons or cords 75 cm (¾ yd) long through the channel, one ribbon entering and exiting on one side, and the other entering and exiting on the other side. Tie the ends together with a knot.

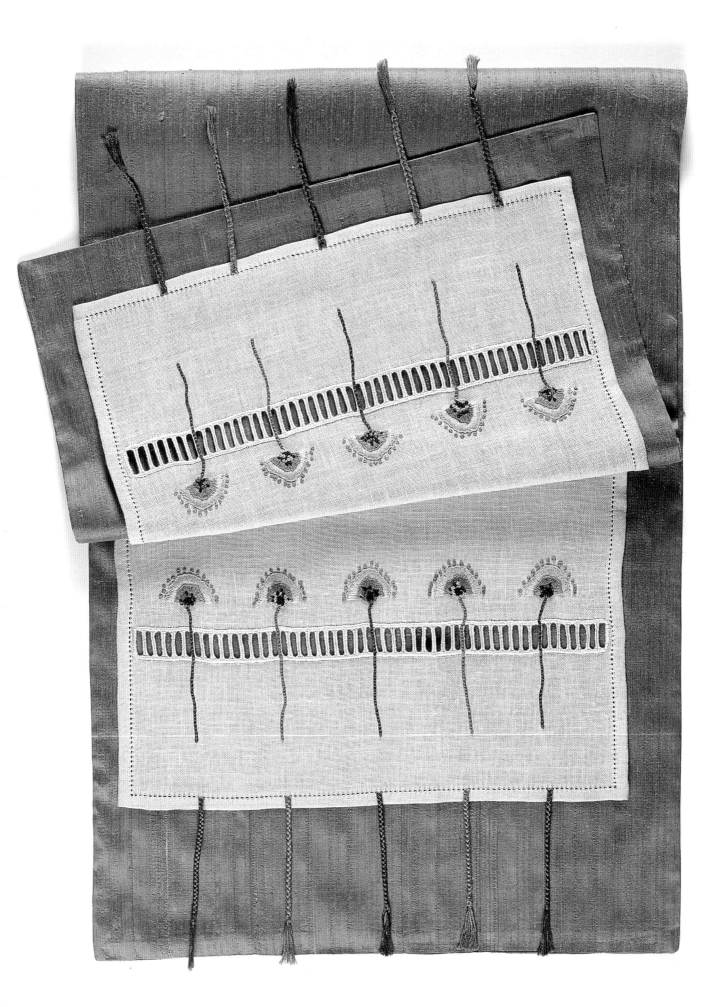

TABLE DECORATION OR RUNNER

This delightful table decoration consists of two layers, an embroidered runner and a silk mat showing colour through the open work border and framing it. Woven borders are edged with satin stitch and decorated with flowers and a fringe of plaited threads. Five colourways are given—the main illustration shows the gold colourway, and the instructions also refer to this colourway. Substitute the threads and fabrics given in the table of page 98 for the other colourways. The length may be extended or reduced to suit your own requirements for a table centre, place mat or even a curtain.

MATERIALS

100 x 45 cm (39½ x 18 in) Belfast linen, 32 count, colour 233 antique ivory

Strips of plain fabric 5 cm (2 in) wide

2 balls DMC perle 8, colour ecru

1 skein DMC perle 5, colour ecru

DMC stranded cotton, 1 skein each:

> *921 copper*
> *976 golden brown medium*
> *3776 mahogany light*
> *3777 terra cotta very dark*
> *3827 golden yellow*

DMC stranded cottons, 2 skeins each:

> *3011 khaki green dark*
> *3012 khaki green medium*

Needles:

> *tapestry needle size 24*
> *embroidery or crewel needle size 5 or 7*

Embroidery hoop

Silk dupion, khaki green, for mat, 2 pieces 112 x 42 cm (44 x 17 in)

Finished sizes:
linen runner 90 x 34 cm (35½ x 13½ in)
silk mat 109.5 x 39.5 cm (43 x 15½ in)

INSTRUCTIONS

Attach plain fabric to the sides of the linen for use with the hoop.

cutting line

hem stitching line

open work

35

satin
stitch border
3 fabric
threads deep

open work 20

9 cm

NOT TO SCALE

Plan of table runner
(not to scale)

On all sides withdraw one fabric thread next to the edge of the fabric, A-B-C-D on diagram. This is the cutting line. On all sides count 35 fabric threads in from the cutting line and cut and withdraw the 36th, E-F-G-H. This is the hem-stitching line.

Borders of satin stitch At both narrow ends measure 9 cm (3½ in) away from the hem-stitching lines E-F and G-H and withdraw one fabric thread, stopping 8 fabric threads away from the hem-stitching lines on the long sides, E-G and F-H, to create I-J. Leave 3 fabric threads and cut and withdraw another fabric thread, parallel to I-J, at K-L. Count 20 fabric threads (open work) and withdraw M-N parallel to K-L, leave 3 fabric threads and withdraw the next O-P, parallel to M-N.

Work satin stitch borders on both borders, between I-J and K-L, and between M-N and O-P, with perle 5.

Don't secure the short edges or cut away ends of fabric threads until after working the woven bars.

Woven bars are worked in the border between the satin stitch edges, with perle 8 over 8 vertical fabric threads, that is, two groups of 4. Several centimetres (a few inches) before reaching the end of the border check the number of vertical fabric threads and incorporate them gradually into the last few woven bars.

Secure the short edges with buttonhole stitch in perle 8.

Embroidery Trace five flowers over the borders, the centre one first, the other stems 6 cm (2¼ in) apart. Work the outer 'petals' (1) with shaded buttonhole in 3 strands 3827, the inner 'petals' (2) with 3

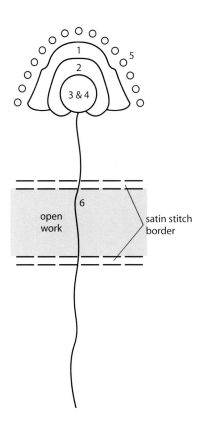

Pattern for flower embroidery in relationship to open work

The five suggested colourways; left to right, blue, violet, pink, neutral, gold

strands 976; fill the centres (3 & 4) with French knots in 6 strands of 921 and 3777; work a random row of French knots (5) outside the 'petals' in 6 strands of 976 and 3776; work the stems (6) in chain stitch, alternating 3011 and 3012.

Hem Cut on the cutting lines to trim excess fabric. Turn the hem and stitch with antique hem stitch using perle 8.

Plaited fringe Alternate colours 3011 and 3012 to make five plaited fringes fixed to the hem below the flower stems.

Silk mat Pin together the two pieces of silk dupion, right sides facing each other. Sew together with a 1 cm (⅜ in) seam allowance and leaving a gap on one side of 14 cm (5½ in). Trim the corners and turn right side out. Stitch the gap closed with ladder stitch and press.

Lay the linen on the silk; do not stitch together.

COLOURWAYS (DMC STRANDED COTTON)

Colours	1. Shaded buttonhole	2. Shaded buttonhole	3. French knots 6 strands	4. French knots 6 strands	5. French knots 6 strands	6. Chain stitch 3 strands	Fabrics
Neutral	Ecru	739	676	ecru	739	3364	Cashel linen sage and cream silk
Violet	333	552	720	742	552	732	Belfast linen 222 cream and purple silk
Pink	899	961	3350	3820	3350	832	Belfast linen 223 ivory and burgundy silk
Gold	3827	976	921	3777	976 and 3776*	3011 and 3012*	Belfast linen 223 ivory and khaki green silk
Blue	341	793	792	783	333	732	Belfast linen 222 cream and midnight blue silk

*Alternate colours in flowers and stems.

SACHETS

The designs and colours of these two sachets, in which you could keep nightwear, handkerchiefs, or even an embroidery project in progress, are reminiscent of old-fashioned English gardens with their picket fences.

MATERIALS

Pink colourway

69 x 35.5 cm (27½ x 14 in) Belfast linen, 32 count, or Cashel, 28 count, colour 333 mushroom

DMC stranded cotton, 1 skein each:

> 223 light shell pink
> 224 very light shell pink
> 316 antique mauve
> 3041 antique violet
> 3740 antique violet dark
> 3859 mushroom pink

Cream and green colourway

69 x 35.5 cm (27½ x 14 in) Belfast linen, 32 count, colour 222 cream

1 ball DMC perle 8 ecru

DMC stranded cotton, 1 skein each:

> white
> ecru
> 613 beige
> 642 beige grey
> 644 beige grey medium
> 739 cream
> 3013 green

Both colourways

Strips of plain fabric 5 cm (2 in) wide

Needles:

> tapestry needle size 24
> crewel or embroidery needle size 5 or 7

Embroidery hoop

Lining fabric 63 x 32 cm (25 x 12½ in)

Finished size 60 x 29 cm (23½ x 11½ in)

INSTRUCTIONS

Attach plain fabric to the sides of the linen for use with the hoop. Tack-mark a rectangle 60 x 29 cm (23½ x 11½ in) in the centre of the fabric. This is the size of the finished sachet.

Border of open work Commencing 5.5 cm (2¼ in) above one narrow end of the fabric, withdraw 22 fabric threads to make a border of open work 18 cm (7 in) wide. Divide the border into groups of 4 fabric threads with four-sided stitch, using 3 strands colour 224 on the pink colourway and perle 8 ecru on the cream and green colourway.

Woven bars Weave bars over two or three groups of fabric threads with 3 strands colour 3859 on the pink colourway and perle 8 ecru on the cream and green colourway.

Secure short edges of borders with buttonhole stitch using 3 strands colour 3859 on the pink colourway and 3 strands ecru on the cream and green colourway.

Embroidery Work buttonhole eyelets and French knots with 3 strands of the colours listed for each colourway, using the photograph for guidance.

Hem Cut and withdraw one fabric thread 11 fabric threads in from the tack-marked edges of the fabric to create the hem-stitching line. Cut and withdraw another fabric thread 32 fabric threads out from the hem-stitching line towards the edge. This is the cutting line. Cut on the cutting line to trim excess fabric. Turn the hem and stitch with antique hem stitch using 3 strands colour 316 (pink colourway) or perle 8 ecru (cream and green colourway).

Lining Fold the edges of the lining fabric over so that they meet the hem-stitching line. Pin to the back of the embroidery and stitch to the hem-stitching line.

Pink colourway Attach 7 plaits around woven bars in all the colours. Make 2 knotted tassels and attach them to the front corners of the sachet. The bodies of the tassels are made from perle 8 colour 3041, and the 3 knotted strings on each one from different colours of stranded cotton.

Cream and green colourway Make 3 knotted tassels and attach one on the left-hand corner, one at the centre of the open work border, and one at the right end. The bodies of the tassels are made from perle 8 ecru, and the 3 knotted strings on each one in different colours of stranded cotton.

Finishing Fold the plain end over for 19 cm (7½ in) and ladder stitch the sides together.

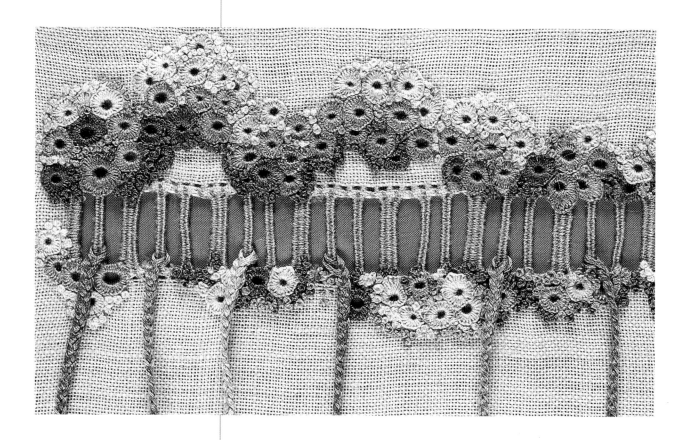

SERVIETTE

The open work border on this pretty serviette is taken from a pattern on a bedsheet in my mother's glory box; the embroidered stars are inspired by the seedpod of the spice star anise.

MATERIALS

45 cm (18 in) square Belfast linen, 32 count, colour 233
  antique ivory

Strips of plain fabric 5 cm (2 in) wide

1 ball DMC perle 8, colour 739 cream

DMC stranded cotton, 1 skein each:
  437 light tan
  738 very light tan
  739 cream

Needles:
  tapestry needle size 24
  crewel needle size 5 or 7
  milliners/straw needle size 3

Embroidery hoop

Finished size 42 cm (16½ in) square

INSTRUCTIONS

Attach plain fabric to the sides of the linen for use with the hoop.

Measure a 42 cm (16½ in) square and withdraw a fabric thread on all sides. This is the cutting line.

Border of four-sided stitch On all sides, count 40 fabric threads in from the cutting line and withdraw one fabric thread, leave 3 fabric threads and withdraw another fabric thread. Work a border of four-sided stitch between these two withdrawn threads with perle 8 in a tapestry needle. (Refer to instructions for four-sided stitch on page 27, and see diagram here for turning a corner.) Work four sides of the corner stitch and make an anchoring stitch at the back of it before commencing with step 2 of four-sided stitch on the next side. The space between the border of four-sided stitch and the cutting line is the fringed area.

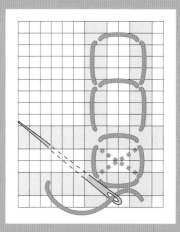

Turning a corner in four-sided stitch border

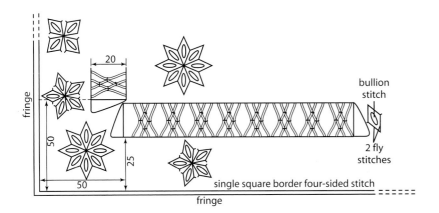

single square border four-sided stitch

fringe

Plan of corner embroidery, open work and stars on serviette

Borders of open work in corner In one corner make an open border 128 fabric threads wide and 20 deep, commencing 25 fabric threads in from the border of four-sided stitch and 50 threads away from the corner (see diagram). Divide fabric threads into 32 groups of 4 with antique hem stitch using perle 8.

Wrapped diamond pattern over 4 groups Eight groups are worked on each border with perle 8.

Secure short edges of border in buttonhole stitch with 3 strands 739.

Repeat for the border at right angles to the first.

Embroidery Follow the diagram for the approximate sizes and placement of the stars. The centre of each diamond-shaped segment of each star is a bullion stitch in colour 437, 3 strands, 12 wraps around a number 3 milliners needle, approximately 8 mm (¼ in) long. Two fly stitches (open chain stitches) are worked to form a diamond shape around each bullion stitch, using 3 strands of 738.

Fringe Cut on the cutting line and remove all the fabric threads to the square border.

DIAMOND AND PEARLS BAG

A square of linen is embroidered and hem-stitched before being made up into a diamond-shaped bag with an embroidered fold at the top. The back and lining are made from silk dupion, and twisted cords draw the bag in at the top. The shape and size of the bag were inspired by an 80-year-old bag from Italy, and the needlewoven pattern by a French reference book of the same period.

MATERIALS

30 cm (12 in) square Belfast linen, 32 count, colour 233 antique ivory

Strips of plain fabric 5 cm (2 in) wide

1 ball DMC perle 8, colour 739 cream

4 skeins DMC stranded cotton colour 739 (2 for cords)

Needles:

tapestry needle size 24

crewel needle size 5 or 7

Embroidery hoop

Assorted pearls and beads

Lining and back of bag, 3 x 22.5 cm (8⅞ in) squares silk dupion

Finished size 19.5 cm (7¾ in) square

INSTRUCTIONS

Attach plain fabric to the sides of the linen for use with the hoop.

Tack-mark a 19.5 cm (7¾ in) square in the centre of the fabric. This indicates the edges of the finished bag.

Double border of open work Make two borders of open work 12 threads deep and 150 threads wide, meeting in one corner and starting 30 fabric threads from the edge of the article. Leave 6 fabric threads (narrow section) and make another border of open work the same size as the first (see Fig. 1).

Fig. 1 Horizontal woven triangles border with corner feature

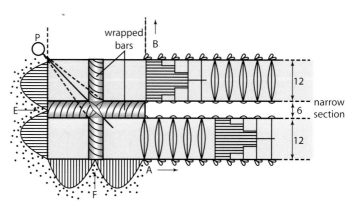

On one of the outer edges of the borders divide the fabric threads into groups of 3 with antique hem stitch and perle 8, working from left to right and starting at outer corner A and inner corner B. Follow with double back stitch border and then complete the opposite sides with antique hem stitch.

Fig. 2 Double back stitch border and crossed bars in corner

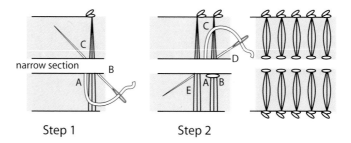

Step 1   Step 2

Work double back stitch with perle 8 over the 6 fabric threads in the narrow section between the two borders, dividing fabric threads into groups of 3 exactly opposite the groups made by antique hem stitch described immediately above.

Working right to left, bring needle and thread out at A, next to the lower edge of the narrow section, 3 fabric threads in from the right-hand edge of the border and opposite the first group of antique hem stitch.

Step 1 Insert needle into B, around the first group of 3, out at C, diagonally across the narrow section and to the left of the first group of 3 fabric threads above it.

Step 2 Insert needle into D, 3 threads horizontally to the right of C, and diagonally across narrow section to E, 3 threads to the left of A.

Repeat these two steps until you reach the crossed bars in the corner. With the same thread wrap across one of the bars, making a half cross-stitch over the centre of the bars, and wrapping to the edge of the corner at E and finishing off the thread.

Complete the other side of the border with double back stitch, starting at the edge of corner F and wrapping the other crossed bar, making a half cross-stitch over the centre of the bars, and continue wrapping to the beginning of the narrow section. Work double back stitch to the end of the border to match the other border.

Decorate the outer edges of the corner with buttonhole stitch with 3 strands cotton and French knots with 6 strands cotton and small pearl beads.

Horizontal woven triangles Refer to Fig. 1. Horizontal woven triangles are worked with perle 8 in the borders over 5 groups of threads, leaving 5 groups unworked between each triangle. Each triangle is worked as follows: Weave backwards and forwards twice over 2 bars, 3 bars and 4 bars, and once over 5 bars (the centre of the triangle), then twice over 4 bars, 3 bars and 2 bars to complete the triangle. Take needle and thread from one triangle to the next under the double back stitches in the middle or under antique hem stitches on the edges.

Arrange the triangles in an alternating pattern in the two borders.

Woven picots in corner Place a pin diagonally from a corner of the square to the middle of the wrapped bars to start each picot, P in Fig. 1. Attach the thread in the middle and work one woven picot in each section of the corner. Remove the pin, twist the picot once and

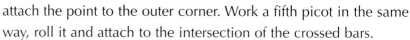

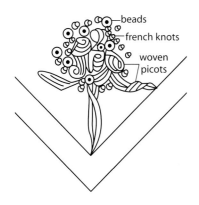

Fig. 3 Embroidery on front corner

attach the point to the outer corner. Work a fifth picot in the same way, roll it and attach to the intersection of the crossed bars.

Front corner Work a freestyle arrangement of woven picot roses and leaves, French knots and beads in the corner opposite the open work but ON THE OTHER SIDE OF THE FABRIC so that it will be visible when folded to the front.

Hem Count 9 fabric threads in from the tack-marked edge and withdraw the 10th. This is the hem-stitching line. Count 30 fabric threads out from the hem-stitching line towards the edge and withdraw the 31st. This is the cutting line. Cut on the cutting line to trim excess fabric. Turn the hem and stitch with antique hem stitch.

Back of bag The back is the same size as the front, and is made and lined from two pieces of silk dupion. Draw the exact shape onto one of the pieces with a pencil. Pin the two pieces of silk together, right sides facing. Sew them together leaving a gap on one side of 5 cm (2 in). Trim the corners and turn right side out. Stitch the gap closed with ladder stitch and press.

Buttonhole bars Work buttonhole bars across both front and back of the bag, starting with one on each side 6 cm (2⅜ in) up from the outer corners, and two between them.

Lining front of bag Fold over one corner of the remaining piece of silk dupion and cut so that the lining commences 5 cm (2 in) in from the two outer corners of the front of the bag and does not cover the embroidered front top fold. Press the other three edges over so that they meet the hem-stitching line. Pin the silk to the back of the embroidery and stitch it to the hem-stitching line and across the corner.

Finishing Join the front and back of the bag together with ladder stitch in sewing cotton, joining the two lower sides, and for 6 cm (2¼ in) on the two upper sides. The unstitched triangular section folds to the back.

Two twisted cords 70 cm (28 in) long are made from 3 x 2 m (2 yd) lengths of stranded colour 739. Thread them through the buttonhole bars, one cord entering and exiting on one side, and the other entering and exiting on the other side. Knot the ends together.

APRICOT POCKET, BAG OR CUSHION

A versatile decorative square that can be lined and used as a pocket on a linen garment, as the front panel of a bag, as the cover of a small cushion or as an insert on a larger one.

MATERIALS

20 cm (8 in) square Belfast linen, 32 count, colour 322 fawn

Strips of plain fabric 5 cm (2 in) wide

1 ball DMC perle 8, colour 739 cream

1 skein DMC perle 5, colour 977 light gold

DMC stranded cotton, 1 skein each:

> *340 blue violet*
> *739 cream*
> *976 medium gold*
> *977 light gold*
> *3827 yellow gold*

Needles:

> *tapestry needle size 24*
> *milliners/straw needle size 3 or 5*
> *crewel needle size 5 or 7*

Embroidery hoop

Lining fabric, 2 pieces 16 cm (6¼ in) square

Finished size approximately 13 cm (5⅛ in) square

INSTRUCTIONS

Attach plain fabric to the sides of the linen for use with the hoop.

Border A square border 22 fabric threads deep is centrally placed on the fabric. Each side of the inner square contains 51 fabric threads divided into 17 groups of 3 with antique hem stitch, using perle 8 colour 739. Work the corresponding outer edges of the border in the same way. Secure the outer edges of the corner squares with buttonhole stitch with 3 strands colour 739.

Woven bars and triangles are worked with perle 5 colour 977. Each woven triangle is made across 13 groups of fabric threads, each woven bar over two groups of fabric threads.

Embroidery Tack-stitch between the 20th and 21st fabric threads out from the border on all four sides—this is the hem-stitching line. Meandering lines of chain stitch with 3 strands colours 976, 977 and 3827 are worked between the border and this line. Bullion stitches, 15 and 12 wraps around size 3 or 5 milliners/straw needle, are worked randomly over the chain stitch with 3 strands colour 340.

Hem Withdraw the tack-stitch and the 21st fabric thread out from the border. This is the hem-stitching line. Count 25 fabric threads away from the hem-stitching line towards the edge and withdraw the 26th. This is the cutting line. Cut on the cutting line to trim excess fabric. Turn the hem and stitch with antique hem stitch using perle 8 colour 739.

Finishing Make four knotted tassels and attach one to each corner. The bodies of the tassels are made from perle 8 colour 739, and four knotted strings on each tassel with colours 340, 976, 977 and 3827.

Lining Fold the edge of the lining fabric over so that the edges meet the hem-stitching line. Pin to the back of the embroidery and stitch to the hem-stitching line. (Omit this step if you are using the panel on a bag or cushion.)

Pocket Attach the square to a coat, dress or skirt, with or without tassels.

Bag Make a bag from silk dupion or other fabric of your choice, and stitch the embroidery, without a lining, to the front as seen in the lime green daisies book bag (page 115).

Cushion Make or buy a cushion the same size or larger, and stitch or tie the embroidery to it without the lining, corners matching or diagonal.

LIME GREEN DAISIES BOOK BAG

S cattered lime green daisies and sky blue woven triangles evoke a fresh spring feeling in a practical utility bag which may be used to carry a book or diary, even light clothing, make-up or a mobile phone.

MATERIALS

28 cm (11 in) square Belfast fabric, 32 count, colour 322 fawn

Strips of plain fabric 5 cm (2 in) wide

1 ball DMC perle 8, colour 739 cream

1 skein DMC perle 5, colour 3760 peacock blue

DMC stranded cotton, 1 skein each:

> *739 cream*
> *597 turquoise*
> *733 olive green*

Needles:

> *tapestry needle size 24*
> *crewel needle size 5 or 7*

Embroidery hoop

Silk dupion, 4 pieces 37 x 23 cm (14½ x 9 in), peacock blue for bag with lining

Finished size of embroidery approximately 18 cm (7 in) square

INSTRUCTIONS

Attach strips of plain fabric on all sides for use with the hoop.

Border A square border 22 fabric threads deep is worked in the centre of the fabric. Each side of the inner square contains 114 fabric threads which are divided into 38 groups of three with antique hem stitch in perle 8 colour 739. Work the corresponding outer sides of the border the same way. Secure the outer edges of the corner squares with buttonhole stitch using 3 strands colour 739.

Woven bars and woven triangles are worked with perle 5 colour 3760. Each woven triangle is made over 13 groups of 3 fabric threads and each woven bar over two groups of fabric threads.

Embroidery Work daisies in detached chain stitch with 3 strands colour 733, and French knot centres with 3 strands in colour 597.

Hem Count 20 fabric threads away from the border and withdraw the 21st. This is the hem-stitching line. Count 25 fabric threads away from the hem-stitching line towards the edge and withdraw the 26th. This is the cutting line. Cut on the cutting line to trim excess fabric.

Turn the hem and stitch with antique hem stitch using perle 8 colour 739.

Finishing Make four knotted tassels and attach one to each corner. The bodies of the tassels are made from perle 8 colour 739, and two knotted strings on each tassel with colours 597 and 733.

Make a rectangular drawstring bag from the silk dupion, approximate finished size 35 x 21 cm (13¼ x 8¼ in), and line it. Attach the embroidery 2 cm (¾ in) up from the base and make 6 buttonhole bars, starting 6 cm (2⅜ in) from the top. Buy ready-made cord or make two 70 cm (28 in) cords from 3 x 2 m (2 yd) lengths of cotton colour 733 (2 skeins). Thread them through the buttonhole bars, one cord entering and exiting on one side, and the other entering and exiting on the other side. Knot the ends together.

WHITE ON WHITE CUSHION, TABLE MAT OR TRAY CLOTH

This embroidery may be used as a decorative top stitched or tied to a cushion or bolster, with a coloured silk mat between them, as shown in the illustration, or used as a table mat or tray cloth with a coloured silk mat beneath it.

MATERIALS

37 cm (14½ in) square Cashel linen, 28 count, colour 222 cream

Strips of plain fabric 5 cm (2 in) wide

DMC perle 8, colour ecru

DMC stranded cotton, 1 skein each:

> ecru
> 738 dark cream
> 739 cream
> B5600 white

Needles:

> tapestry needle size 24
> crewel or embroidery needle size 5 or 7

Embroidery frame (preferable) or hoop

Finished size approximately 28 cm (11 in) square

INSTRUCTIONS

Attach fabric to a frame or attach plain fabric to the sides of the linen for use with the hoop.

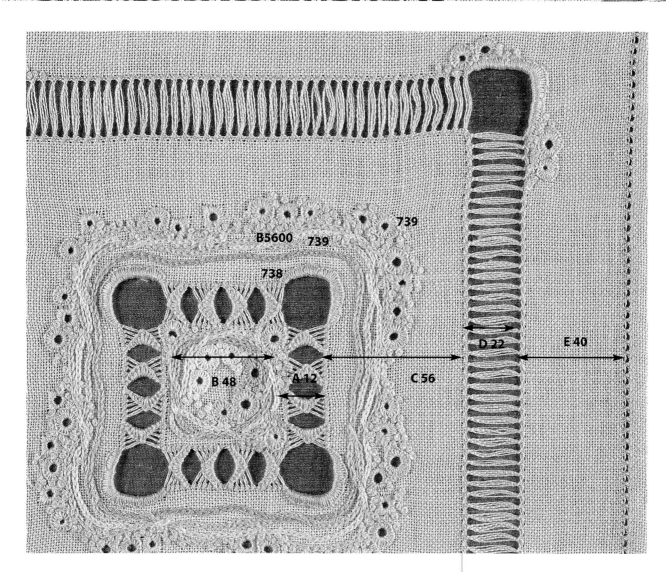

Detail and plan of borders and embroidery

Inner border The central square border is 12 fabric threads deep, A in the detail photograph. Each side of the inner square, B, contains 48 fabric threads divided into 24 groups of 2 fabric threads with antique hem stitch using perle 8. Work the corresponding outer sides of this border the same way.

Four buttonhole triangles are worked in each side with 3 strands 739. The two centre ones mirror image, and the other two pointing towards the corners. Secure the outer edges of the corners with buttonhole stitch with 3 strands 739.

Outer border The outer square border is 56 fabric threads, C, away from the centre square border, and 22 fabric threads deep, D. Fabric threads are divided into groups of 4 with antique hem stitch and perle 8 on both edges. Secure the outer edges of the open corners with buttonhole stitch using 3 strands colour 739.

Embroidery Embroidery stitches are all made with 3 strands thread. The meandering lines of chain stitch within the central square and around the inner border are worked in all colours. The buttonhole eyelets and French knots within the central square are worked in all colours, those around the inner and outer borders in ecru. Apply these stitches following the model or create your own patterns.

Hem Count 40 fabric threads away from the outer square border, E, and withdraw the 41st thread. This is the hem-stitching line. Count 25 threads away from the hem-stitching line and withdraw the 26th. This is the cutting line. Cut on the cutting line to trim excess fabric. Turn the hem and stitch with antique hem stitch using perle 8.

Finishing Attach a knotted tassel to each corner. The bodies of the tassels are made with perle 8, and the three knotted strings on each tassel from white, 739 and 738.

Mat Hem a 37 cm (14½ in) square of silk dupion to finished size 33 cm (13 in) square.

Cushion Attach the embroidery with ribbons or stitching, with or without the mat, to a cushion.

Table mat or tray cloth Place the embroidery on top of the mat.